FOR ORGANS, PIANOS & ELECTRONIC KEYBOARDS

110

the **NEIL DIAMOND** collection

E-Z Play TODAY chord notation is designed for playing **standard chord positions** or **single key chords** on all **major brand organs** and **portable keyboards**.

T0071673

Contents

7777 W. BLUEMOUND RD. P.O. BOX 13819 MILWAUKEE, WI 53213

Cover photo: John Byrson

America

From the Motion Picture "The Jazz Singer"

Registration 4
Rhythm: Rock

Words and Music by
Neil Diamond

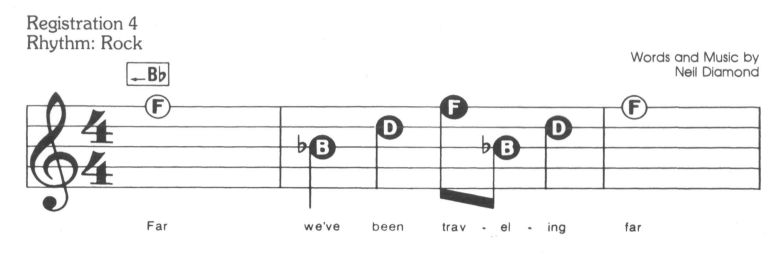

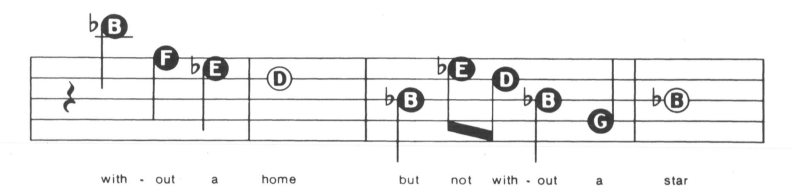

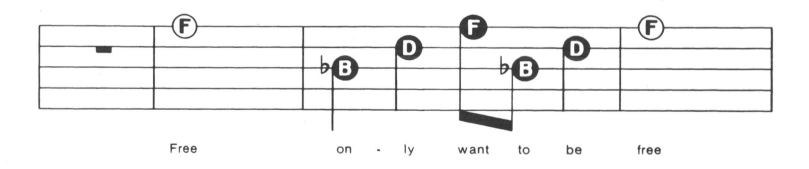

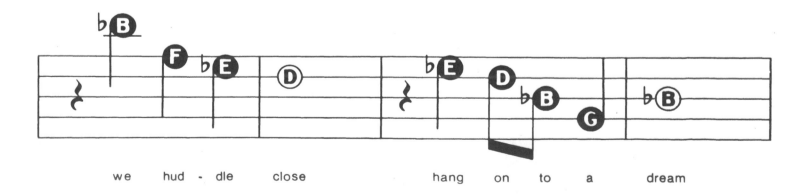

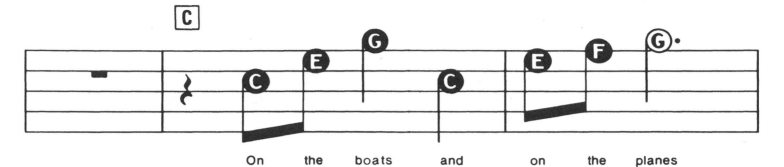

On the boats and on the planes

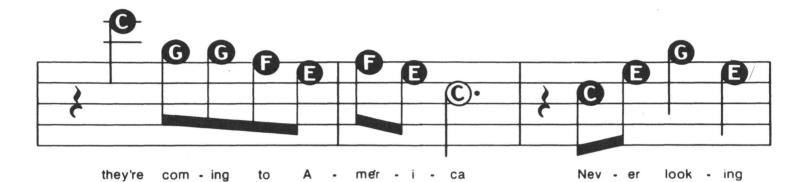

they're com - ing to A - mer - i - ca   Nev - er look - ing

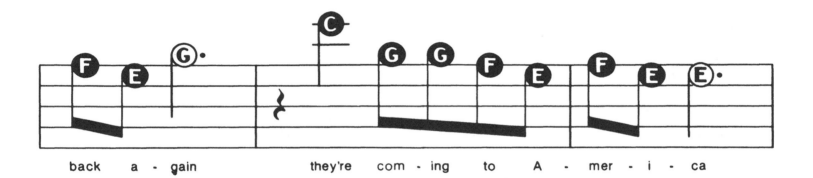

back a - gain   they're com - ing to A - mer - i - ca

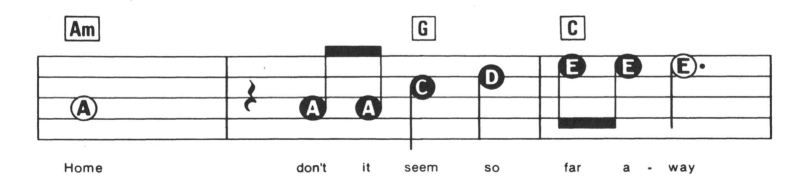

Home   don't it seem so far a - way

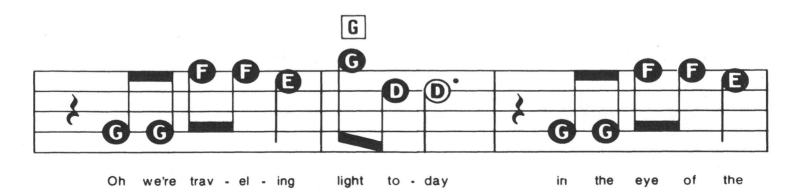

Oh we're trav - el - ing light to - day   in the eye of the

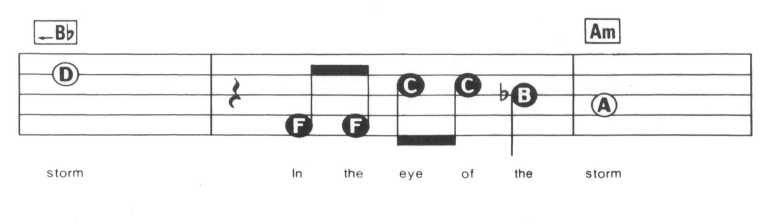

storm — In the eye of the storm

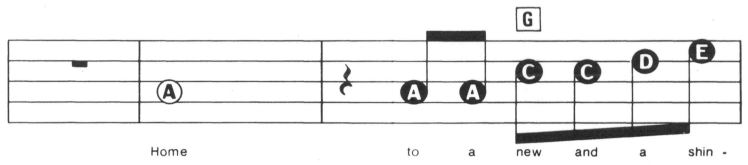

Home — to a new and a shin -

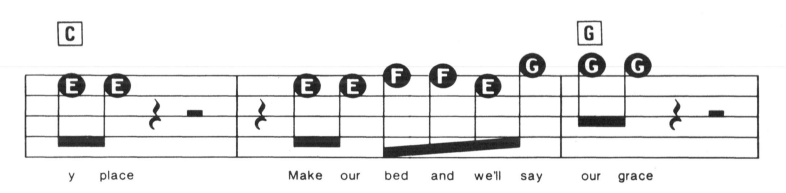

y place — Make our bed and we'll say our grace

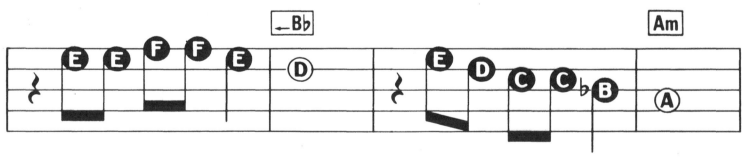

Free-dom's light burn - ing warm — Free-dom's light burn - ing warm

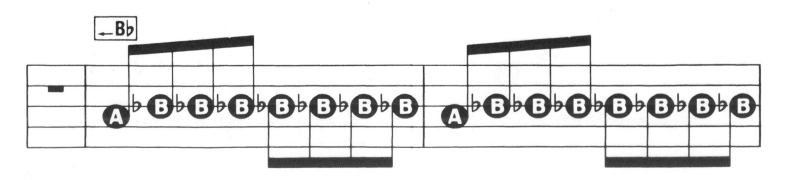

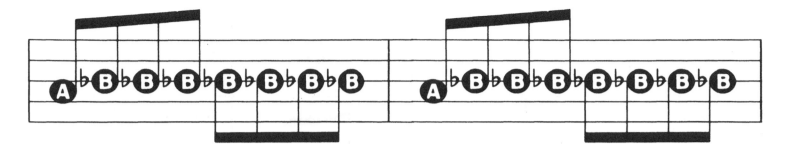

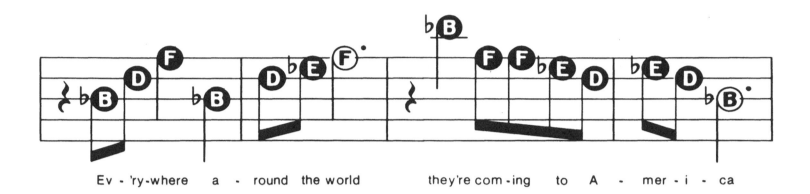

Ev - 'ry-where a - round the world   they're com -ing to A - mer - i - ca

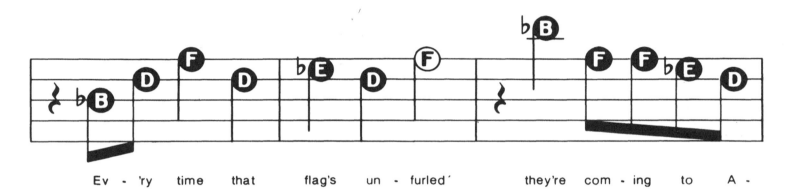

Ev - 'ry time that   flag's un - furled'   they're com - ing to A -

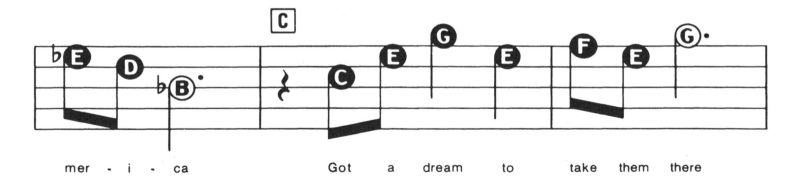

mer - i - ca   Got   a   dream   to   take   them   there

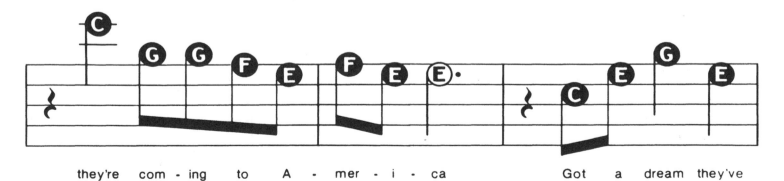

they're com - ing   to   A - mer - i - ca   Got   a   dream they've

6

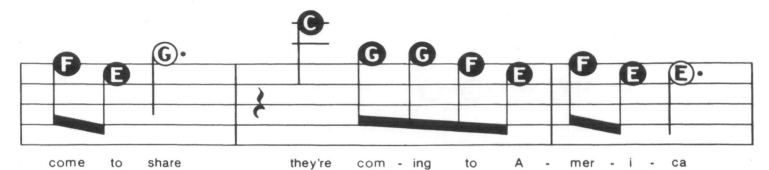

come to share   they're com - ing to A - mer - i - ca

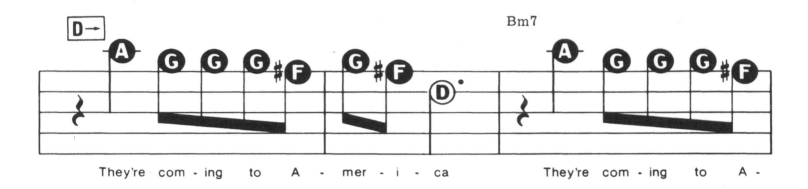

They're com - ing to A - mer - i - ca   They're com - ing to A -

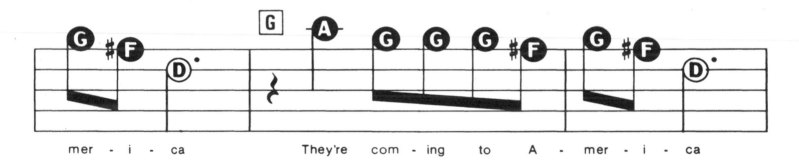

mer - i - ca   They're com - ing to A - mer - i - ca

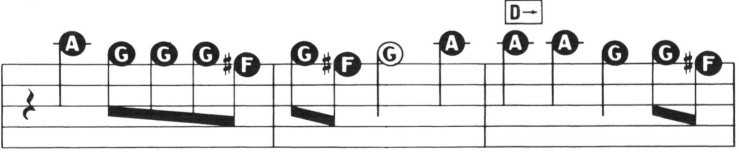

They're com - ing to A - mer - i - ca To - day

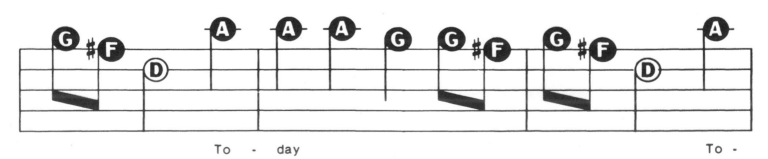

To - day   To -

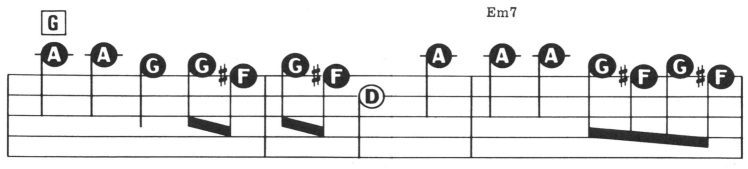

day · · · · · · To - day

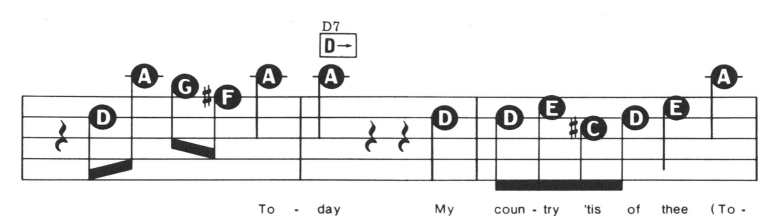

To - day · · My · coun - try 'tis of thee (To -

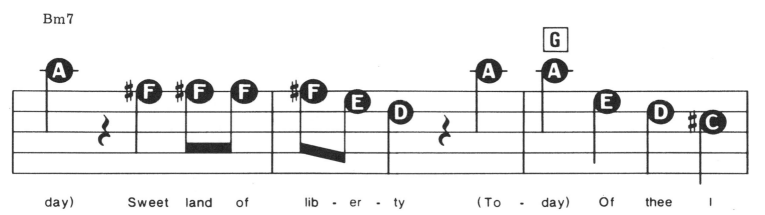

day) · Sweet land of lib - er - ty · (To - day) · Of · thee · I

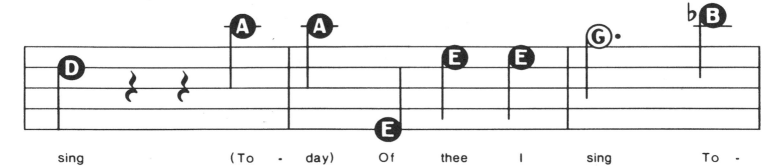

sing · · · (To - day) · Of · thee · I · sing · · To -

Repeat and Fade

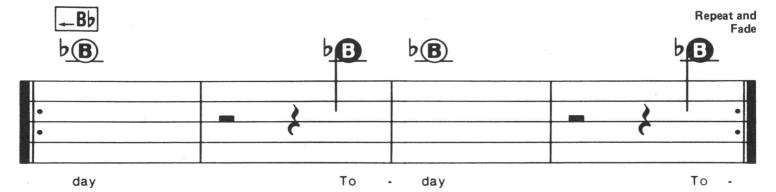

day · · · · To - day · · · · To -

Be Mine Tonight

Registration 1
Rhythm: Rock or Latin

Words and Music by Neil Diamond

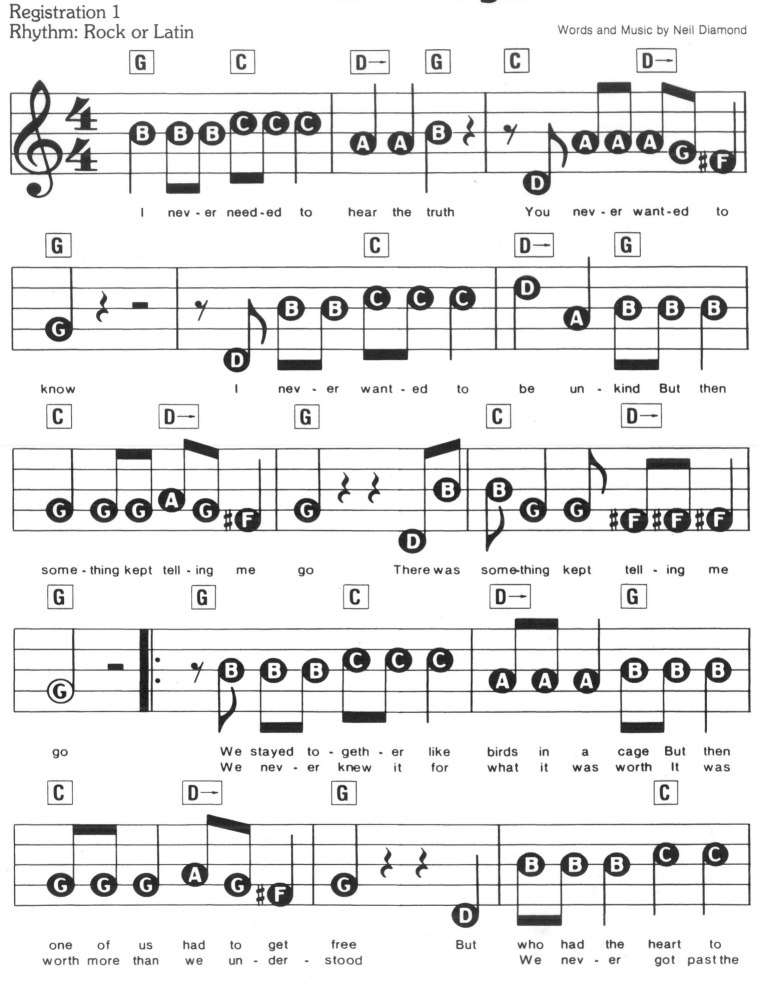

9

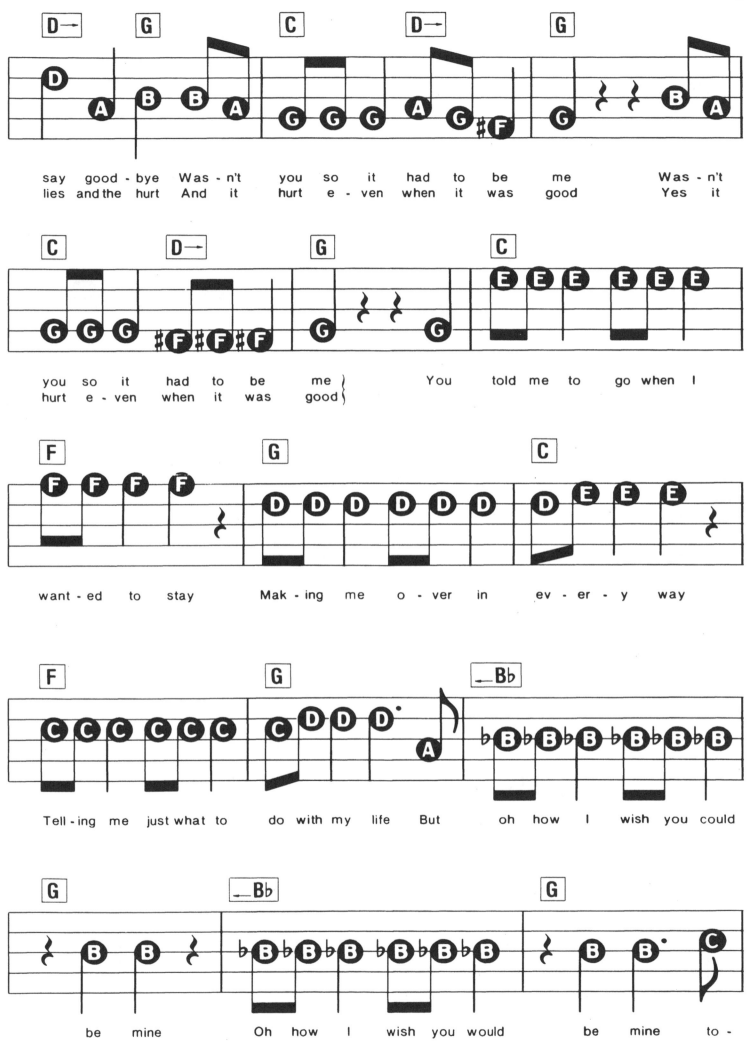

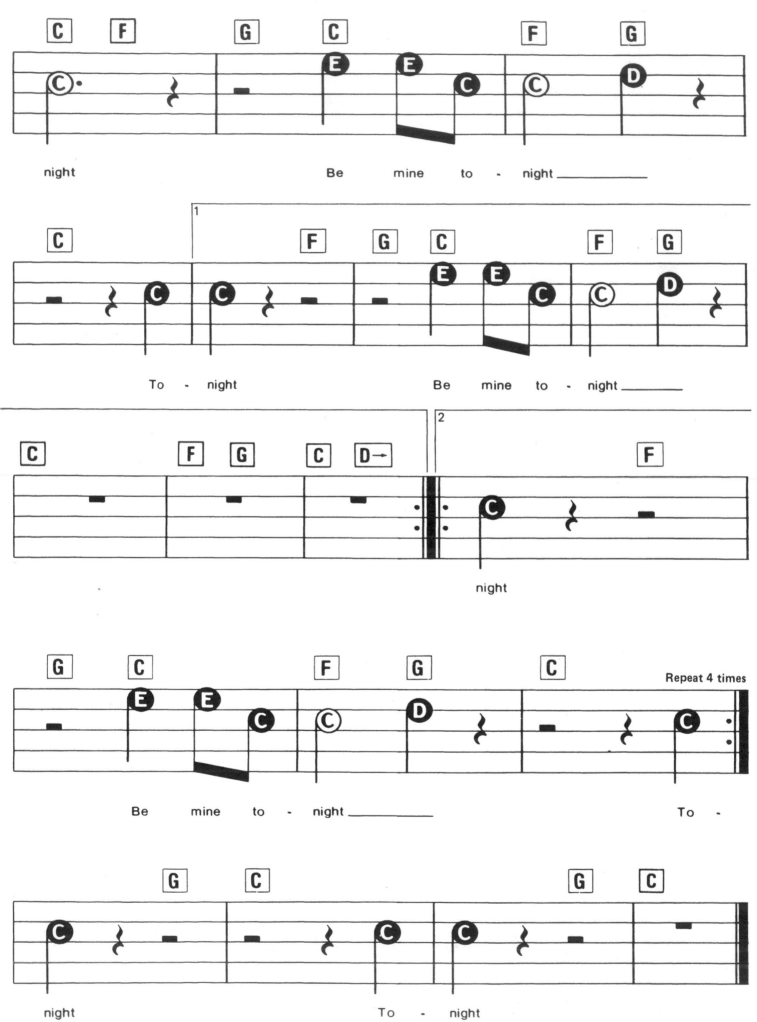

Cherry, Cherry

Registration 9
Rhythm: Ballad or Fox Trot

Words and Music by
Neil Diamond

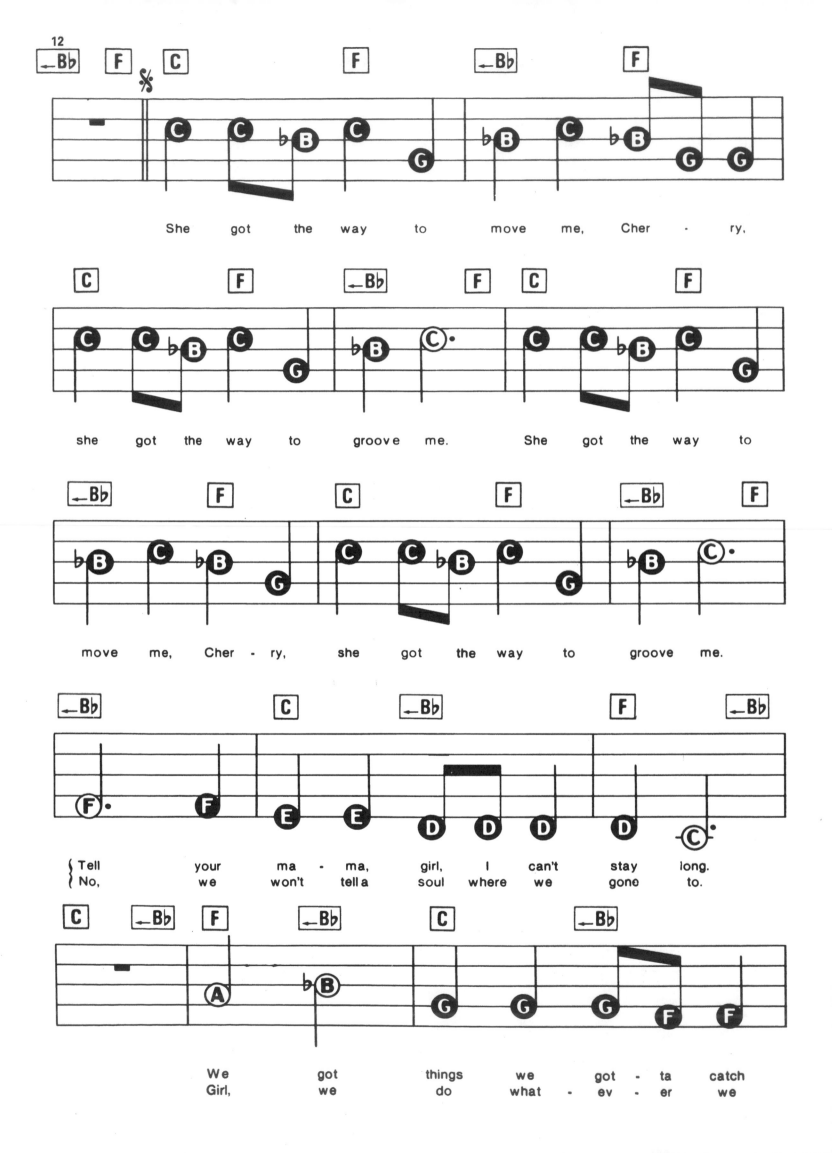

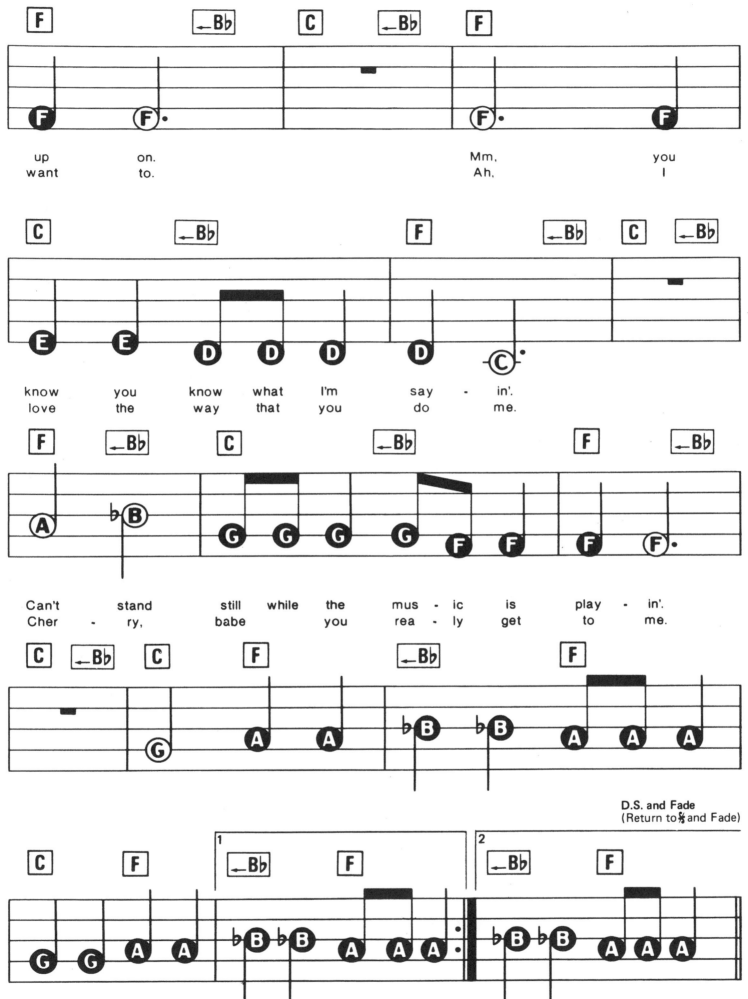

Beautiful Noise

Registration 2
Rhythm: Rock or Fox Trot

Words and Music by
Neil Diamond

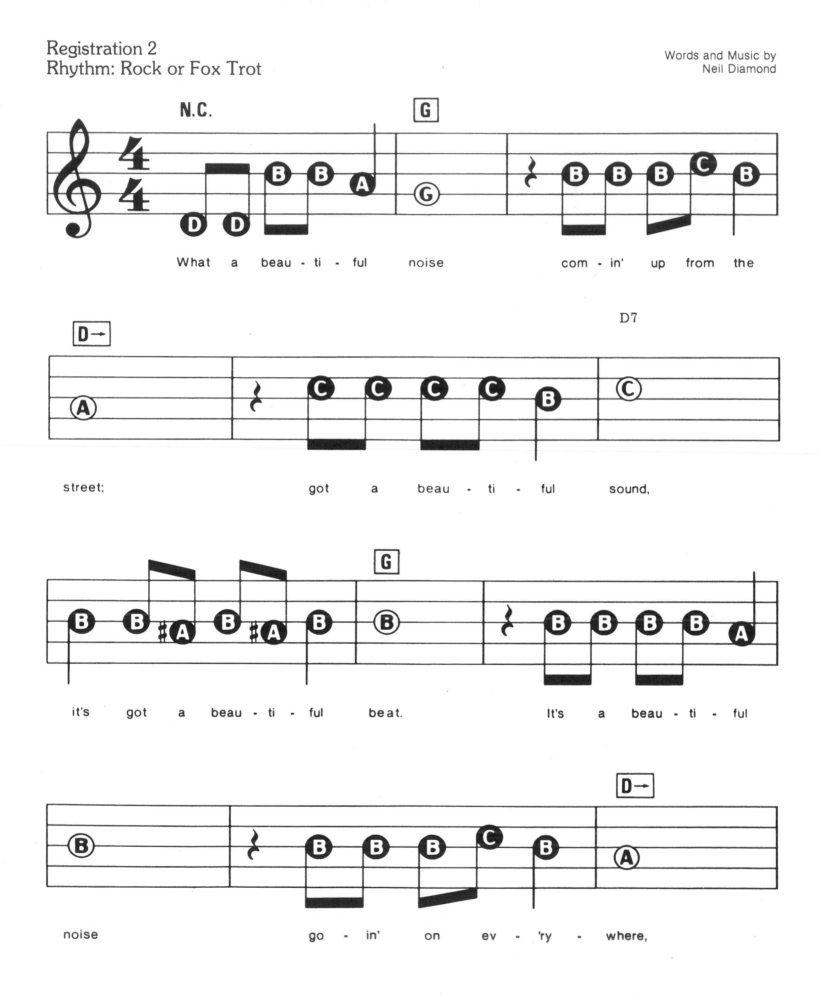

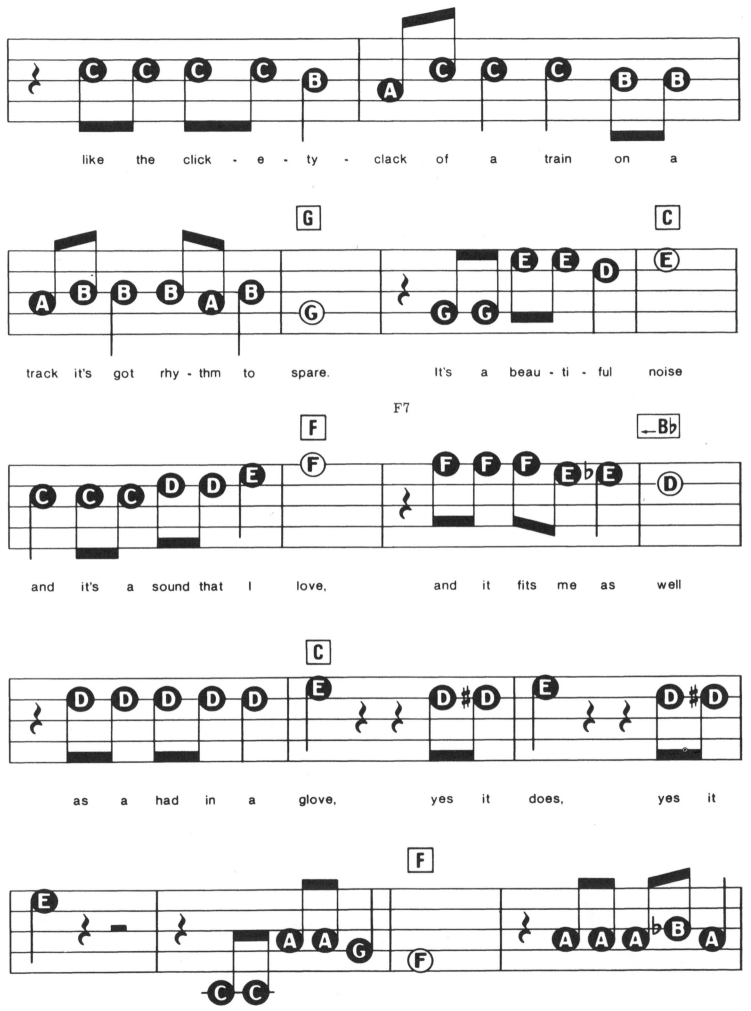

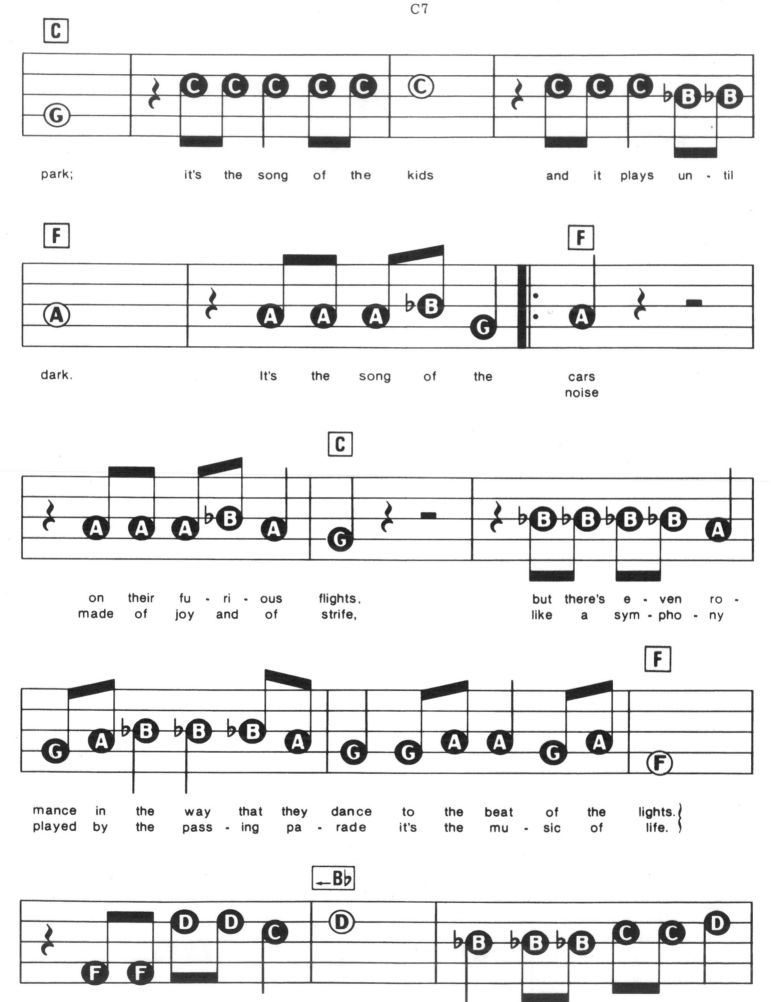

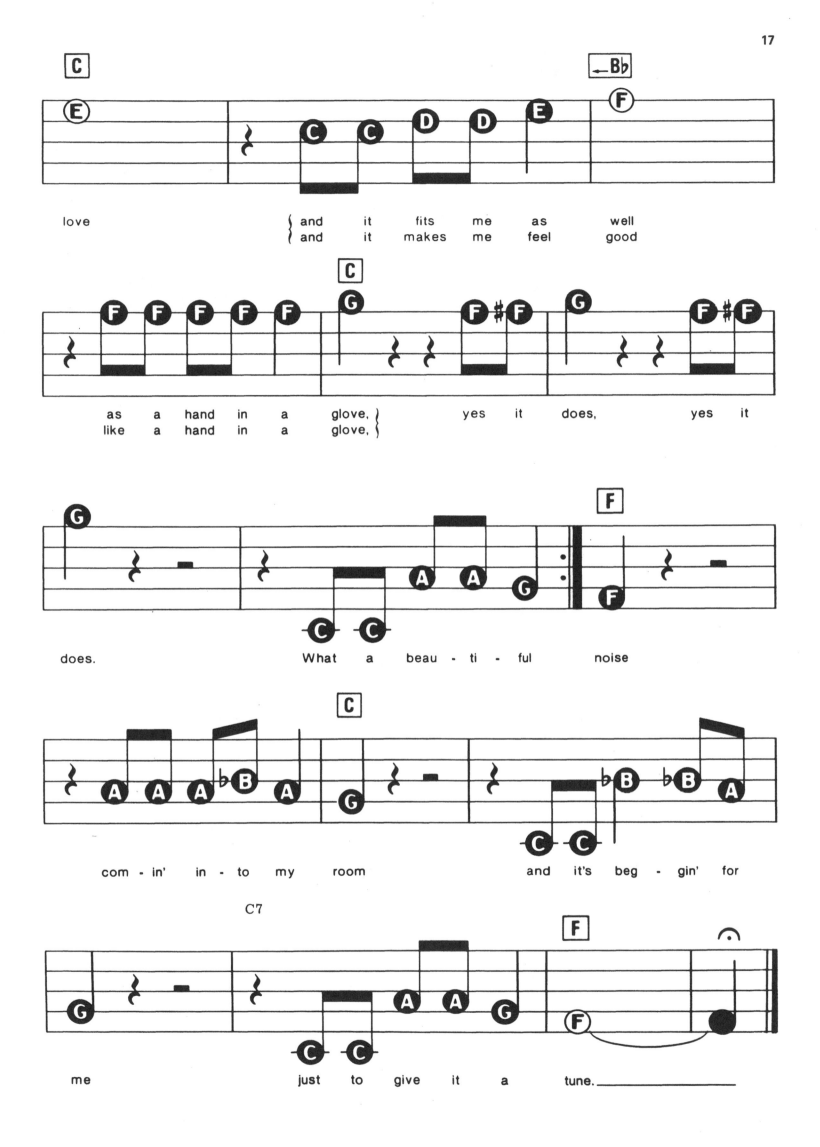

Brooklyn Roads

Registration 4
Rhythm: Fox Trot or Rock

Words and Music by
Diamond

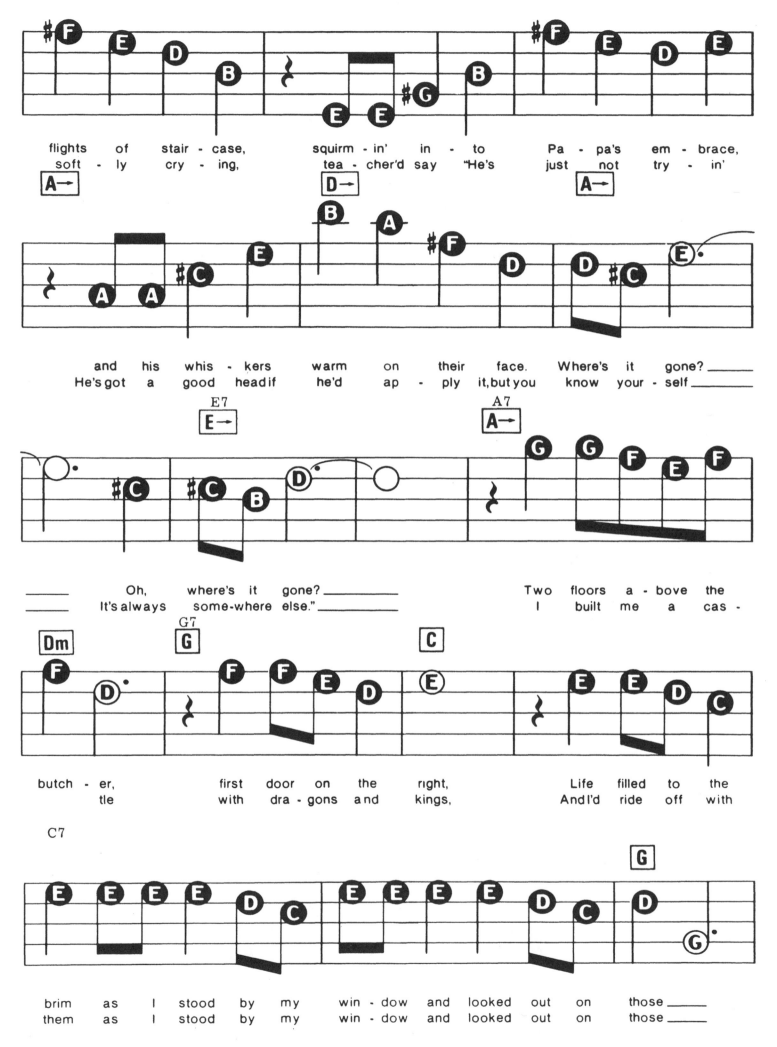

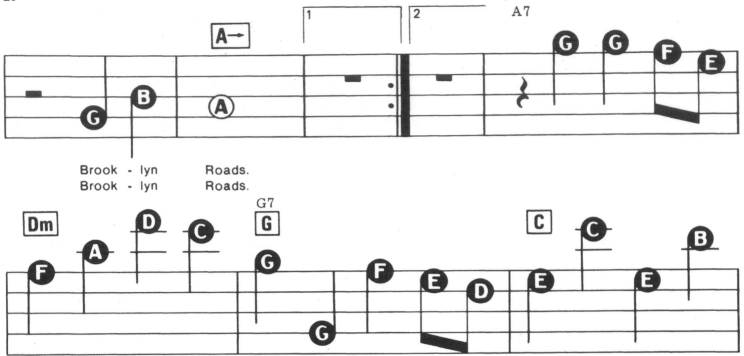

Brook - lyn   Roads.
Brook - lyn   Roads.

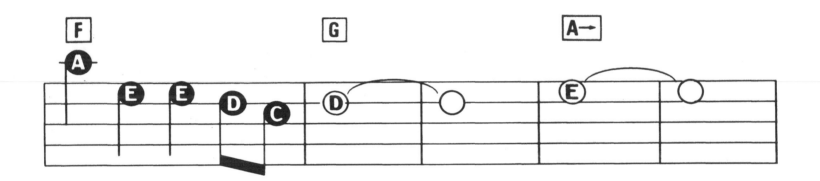

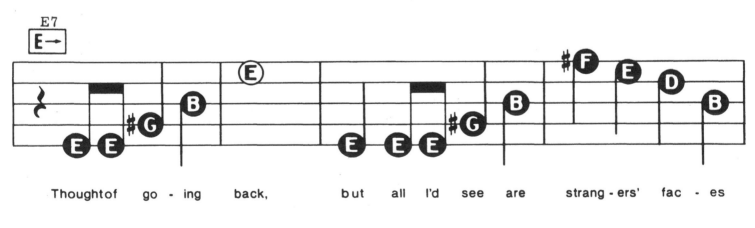

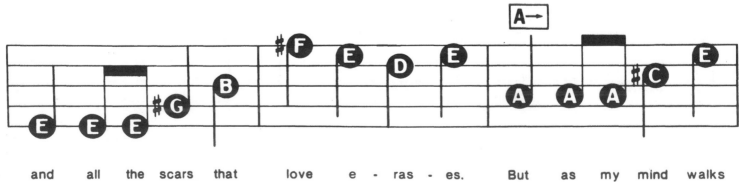

Thought of go - ing back,   but all I'd see are strang - ers' fac - es

and all the scars that love e - ras - es.   But as my mind walks

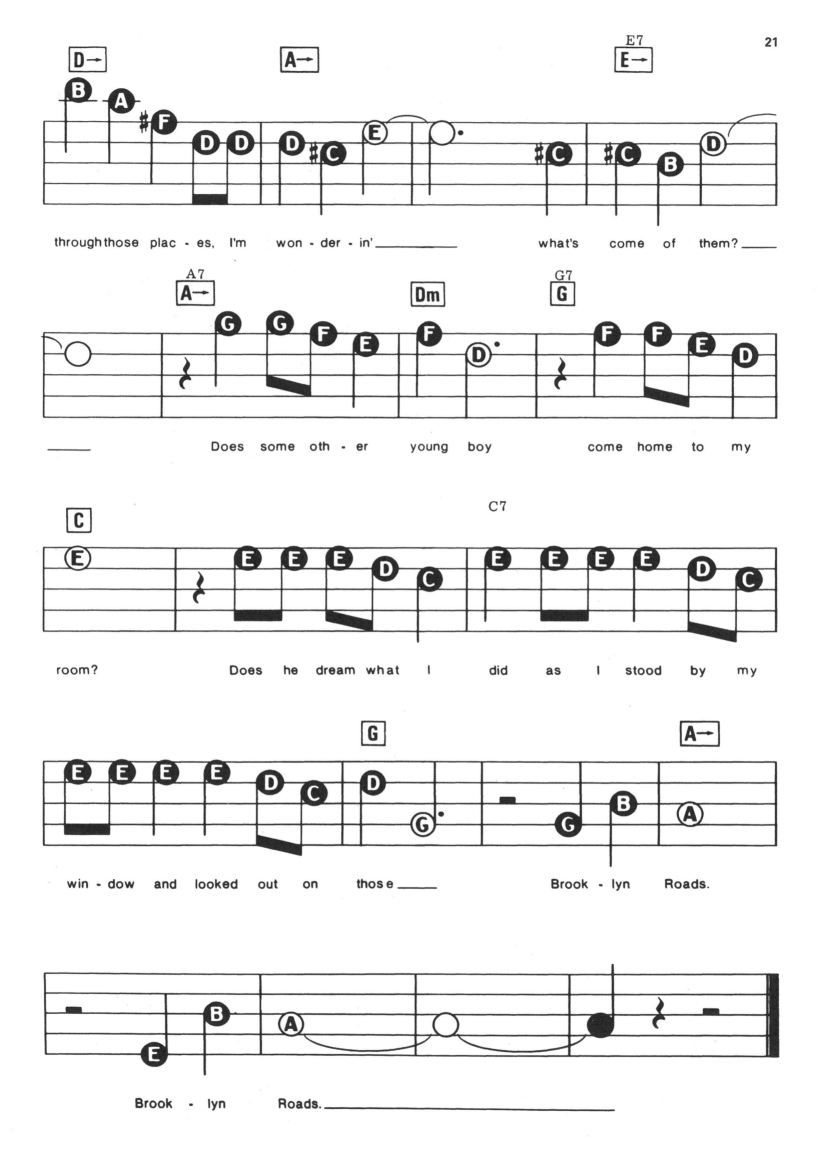

Brother Love's Traveling Salvation Show

Registration 2
Rhythm: Gospel or Fox Trot

Words and Music by
Neil Diamond

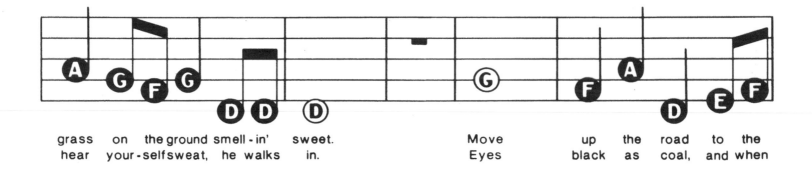

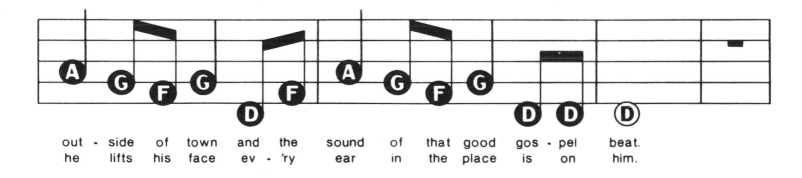

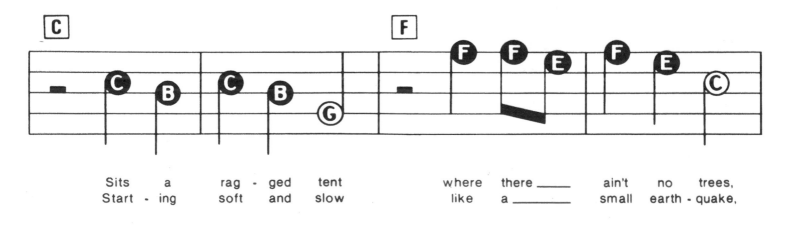

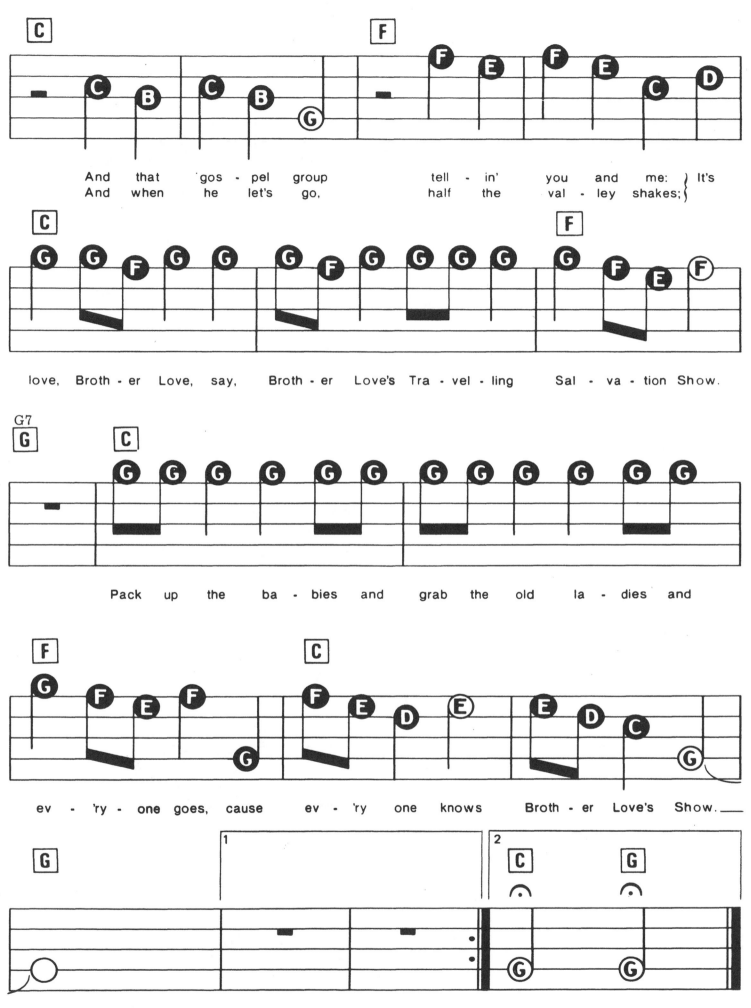

And that 'gos - pel group   tell - in' you and me: ⎱ It's
And when he let's go,   half the val - ley shakes; ⎰

love, Broth - er Love, say, Broth - er Love's Tra - vel - ling Sal - va - tion Show.

Pack up the ba - bies and grab the old la - dies and

ev - 'ry - one goes, cause ev - 'ry one knows Broth - er Love's Show.____

____   A - men.

Comin' Home

Registration 4
Rhythm: Rock

Words and Music by Neil Diamond.

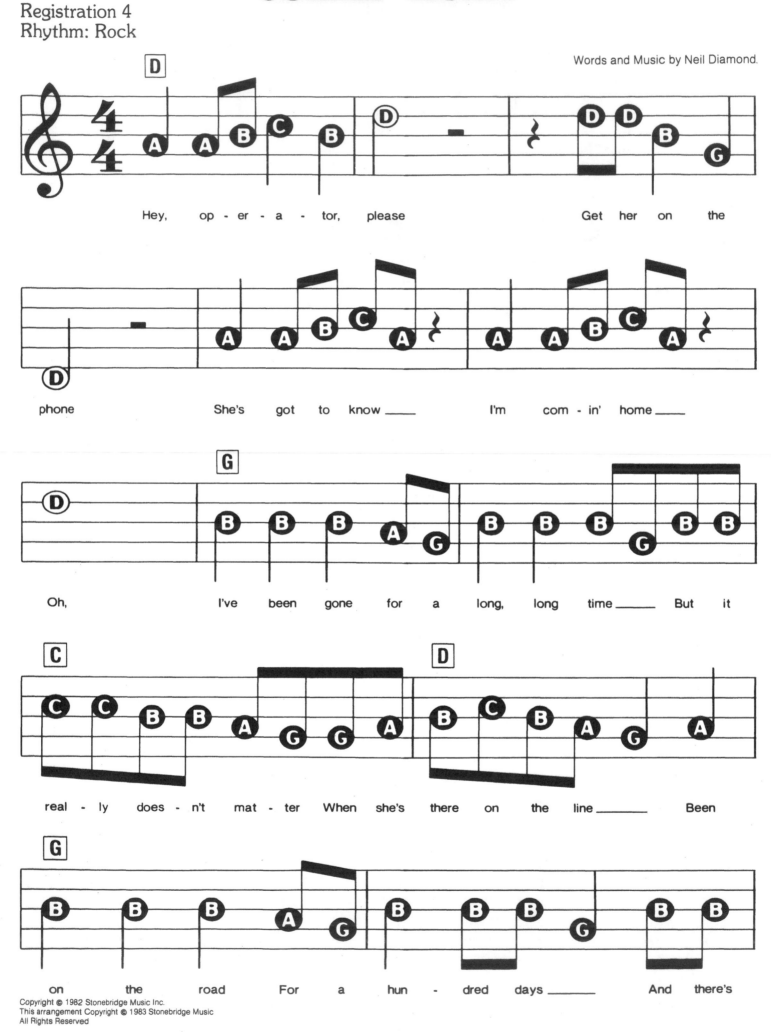

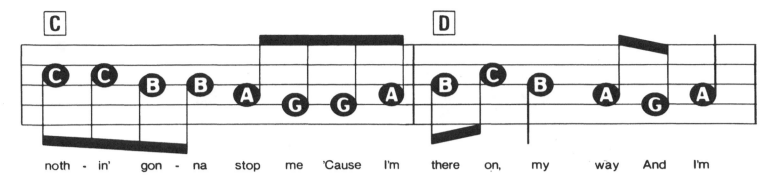

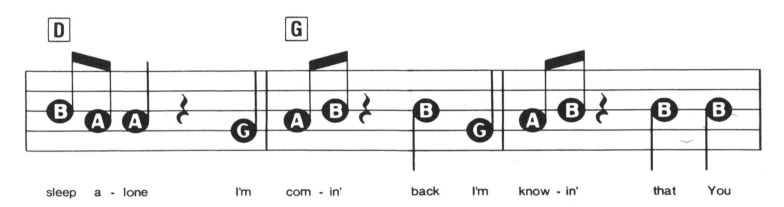

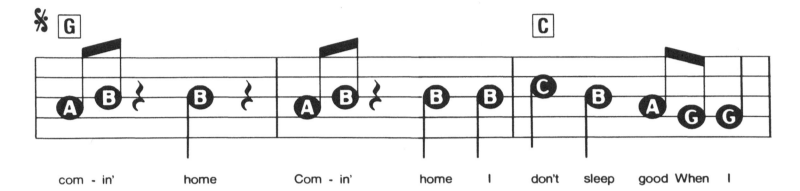

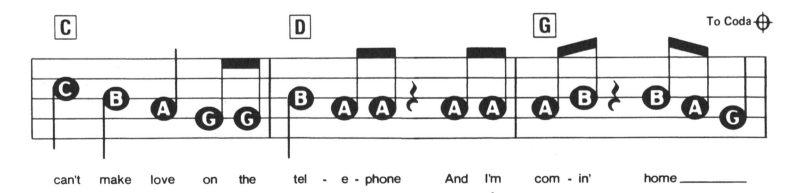

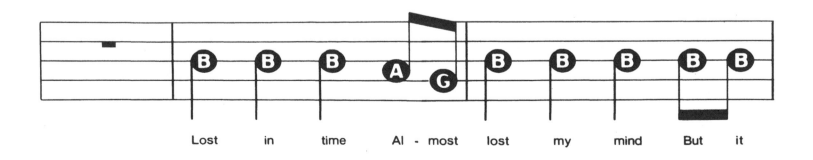

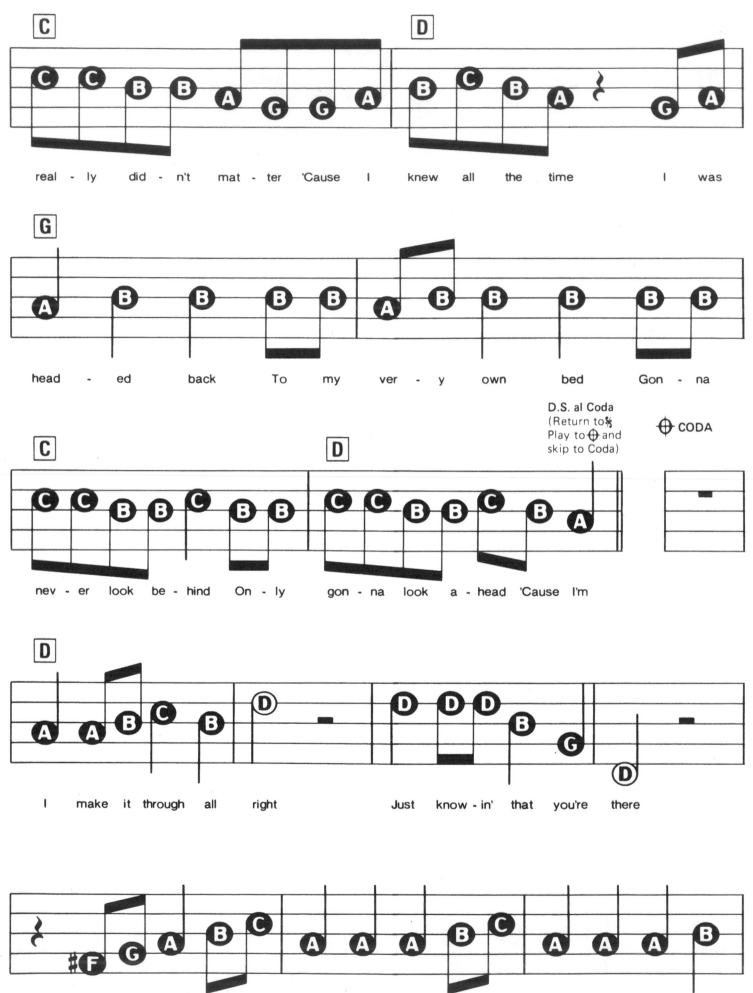

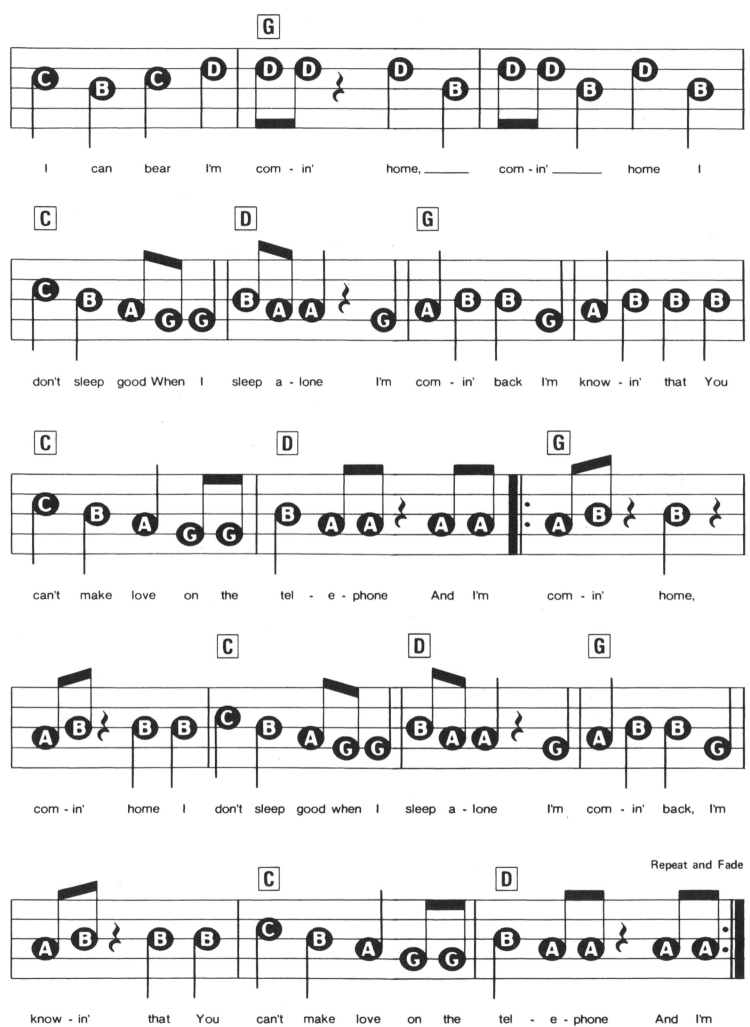

Repeat and Fade

Cracklin' Rosie

Registration 5
Rhythm: Fox Trot or Ballad

Words and Music by
Neil Diamond

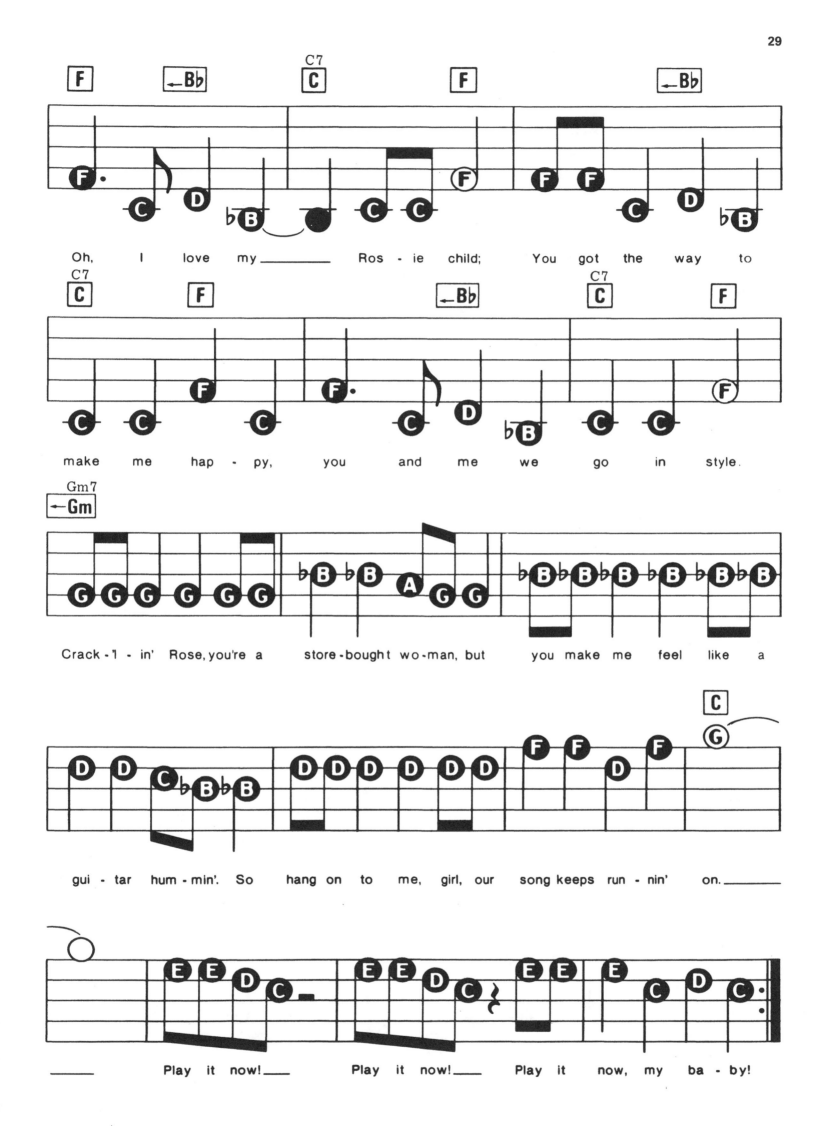

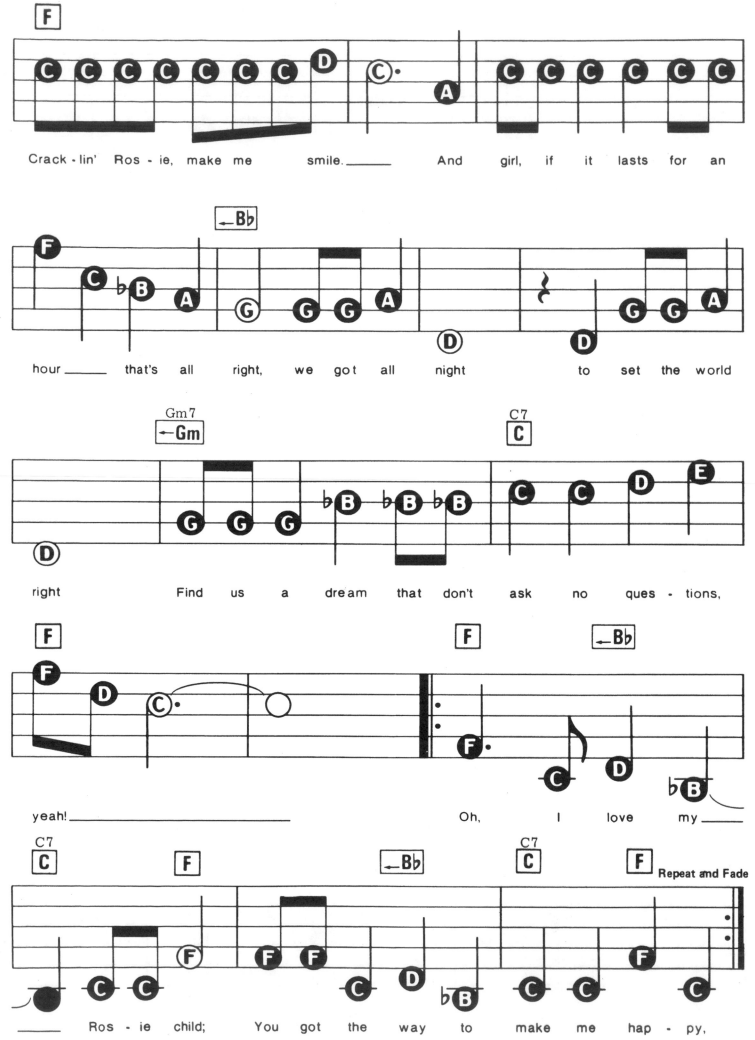

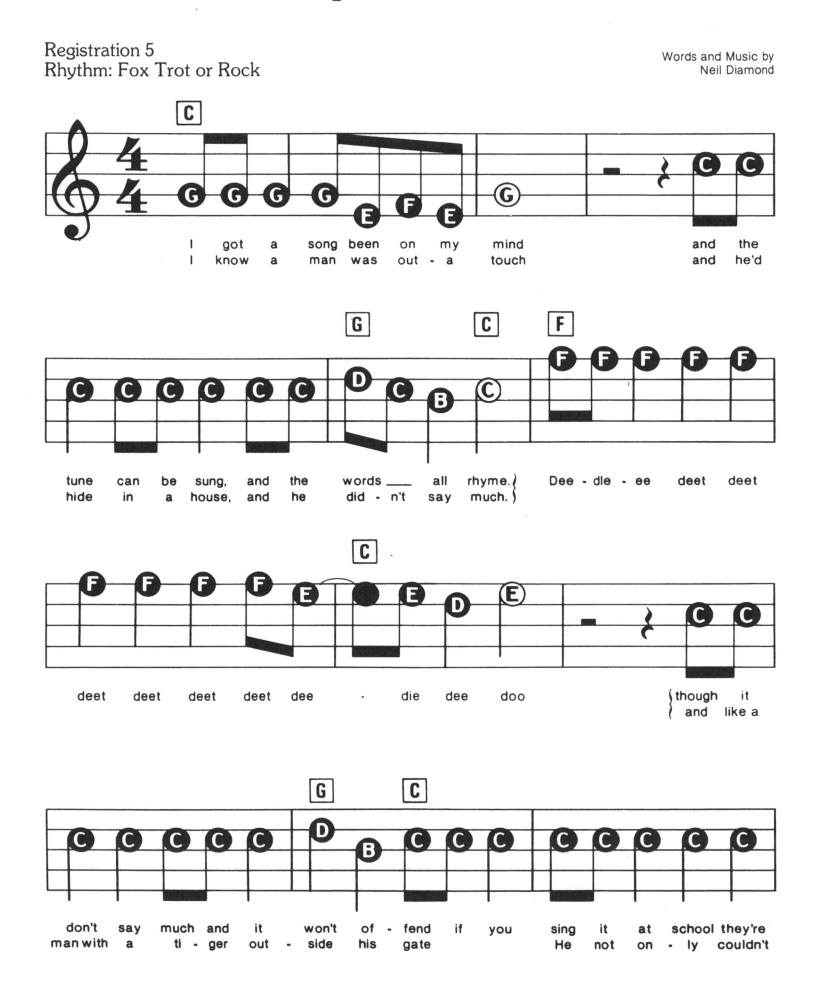

Crunchy Granola Suite

Registration 5
Rhythm: Fox Trot or Rock

Words and Music by
Neil Diamond

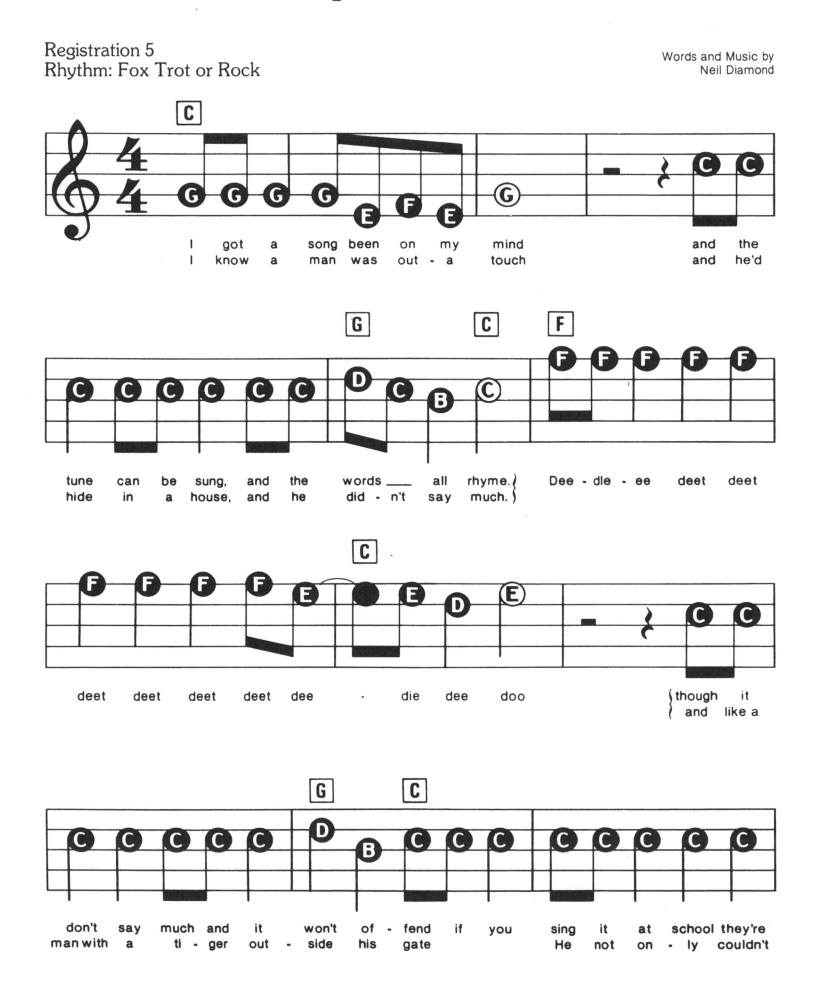

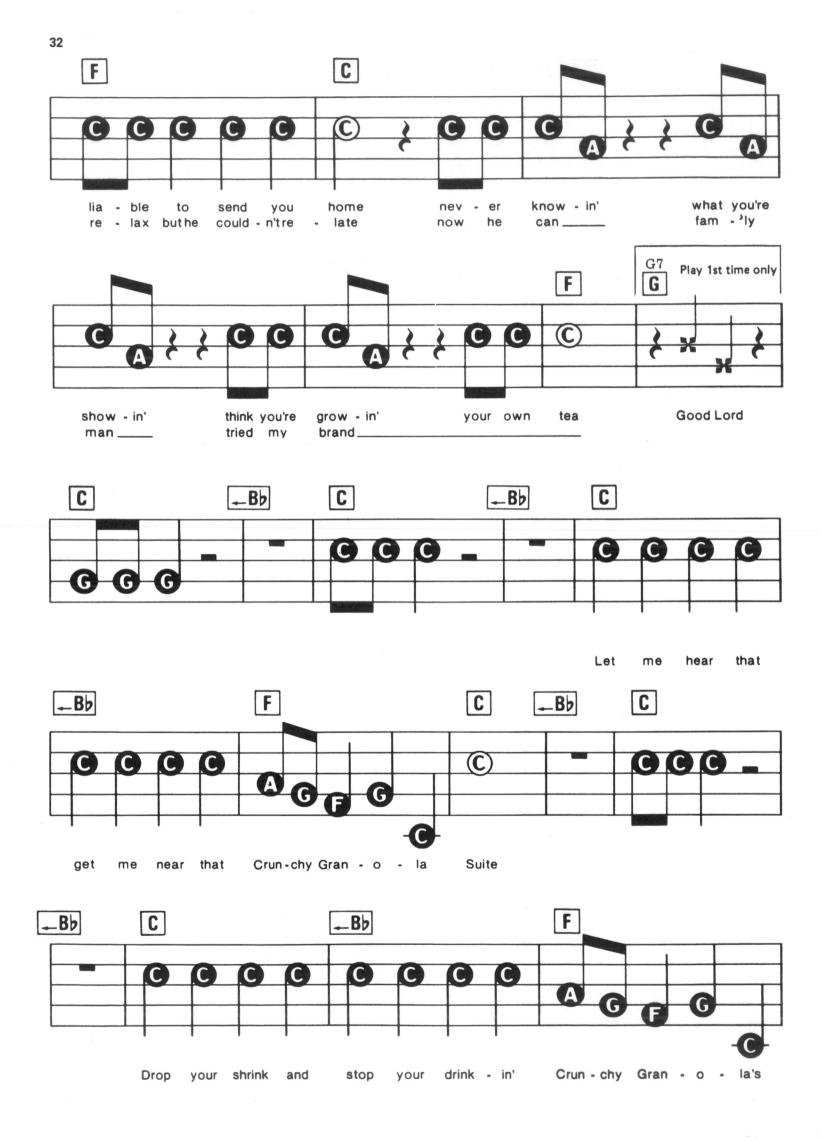

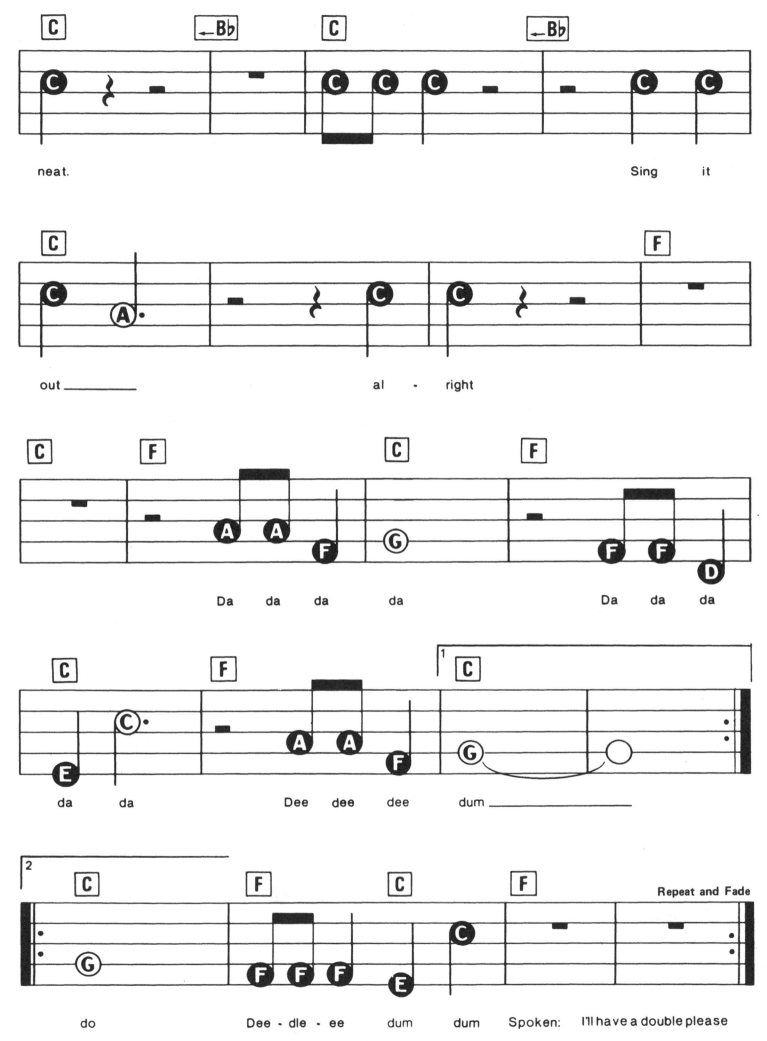

Desirée

Registration 2
Rhythm: Ballad or Fox Trot

Words and Music by
Neil Diamond

It was the third of June on the young-er day
fourth of June on the sleep-less night

Well, I be - came a man at the hands of a girl al - most
Well, I tossed and I turned while the thought of her burned up and

twice my age. And she came to me just like a
down my mind. For she was there and gone with - out

morn - 'ing sun, and it was - n't so much her
one re - gret, but she con - tin - ues on like the

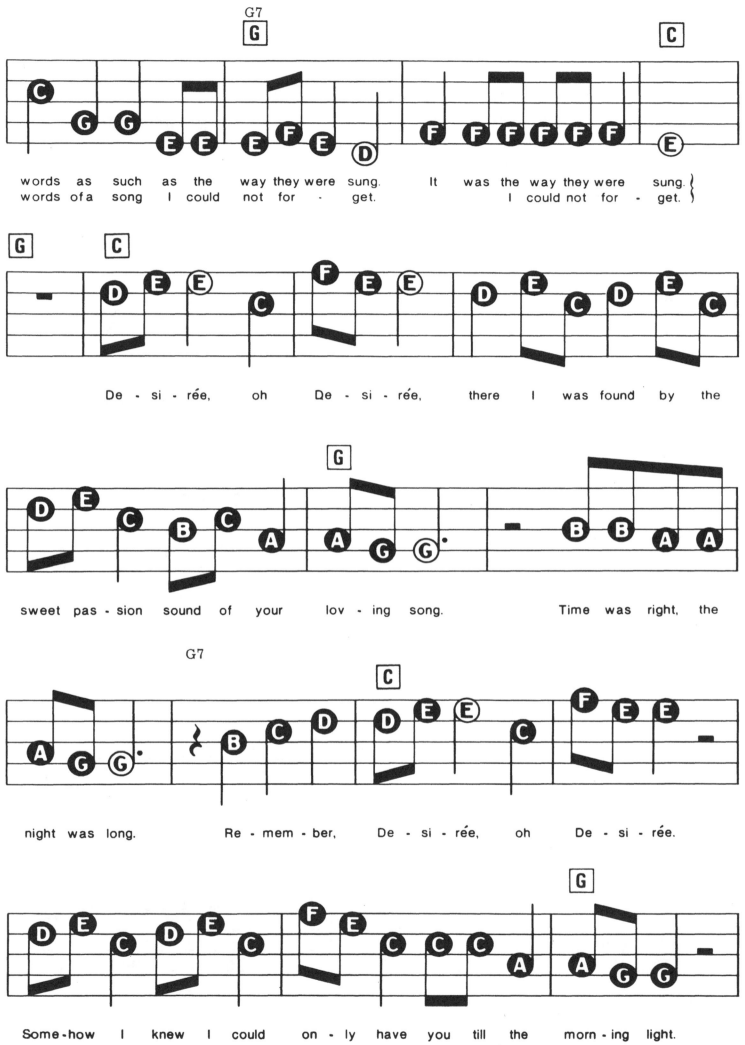

36

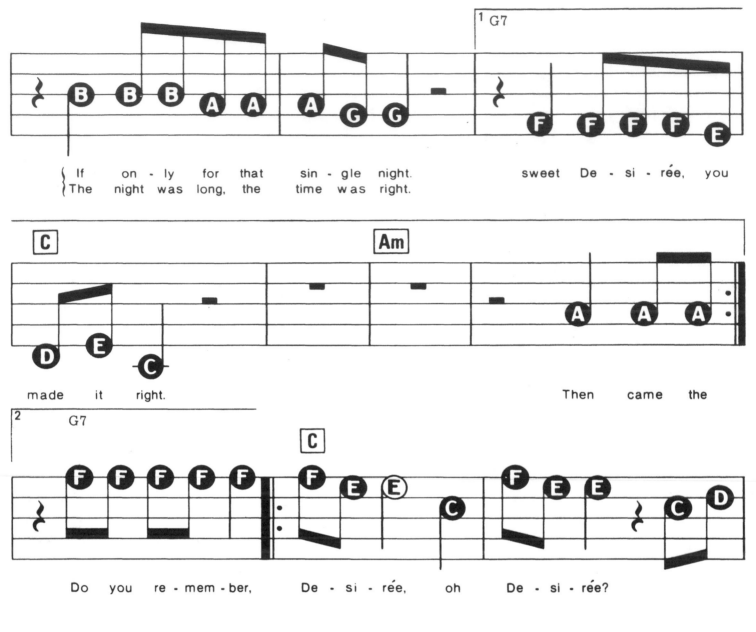

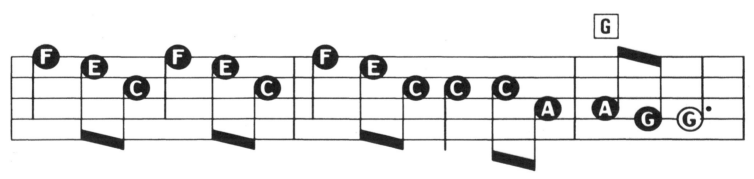

Heartlight

Registration 4
Rhythm: Ballad

Words and Music by Neil Diamond,
Burt Bacharach and Carole Bayer Sager

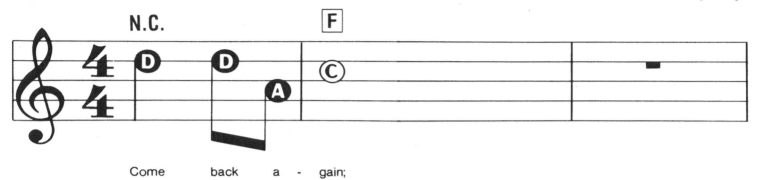

Come back a - gain;

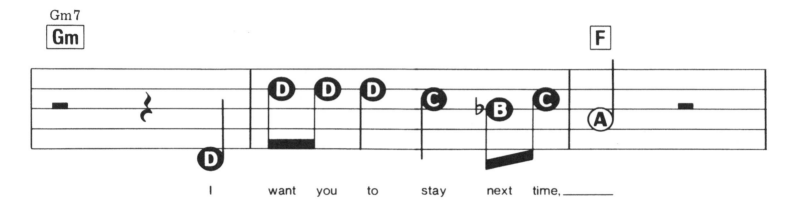

I want you to stay next time,_____

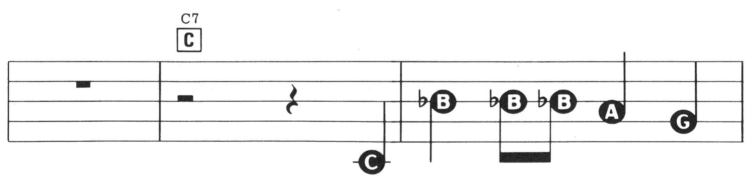

'Cause some - times the world ain't

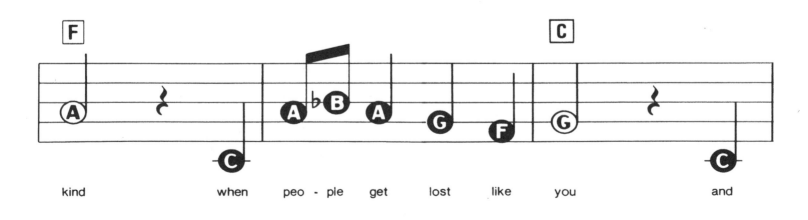

kind when peo - ple get lost like you and

38

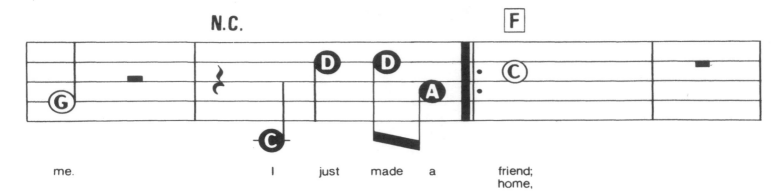

N.C.

F

me.

I just made a friend;
home,

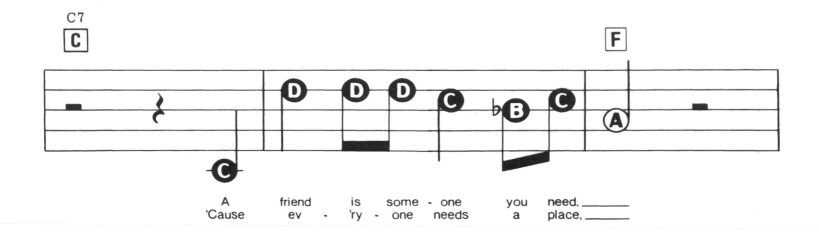

C7
C

F

A friend is some - one you need, _____
'Cause ev - 'ry - one needs a place, _____

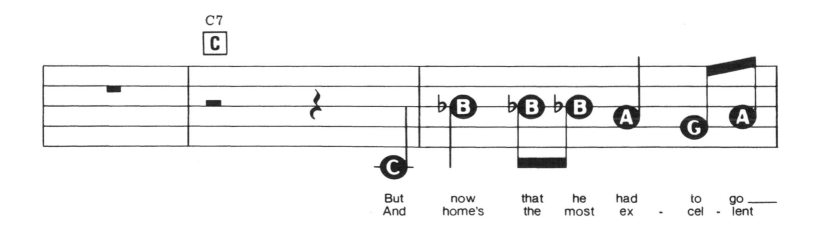

C7
C

But now that he had to go _____
And now home's the most ex - cel - lent

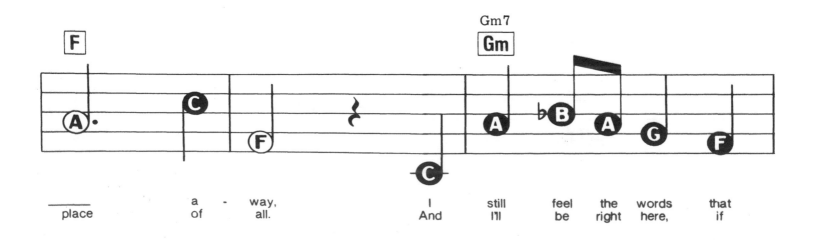

F

Gm7
Gm

_____ place a - way,
place of all.

I still feel the words, that
And I'll be right here, if

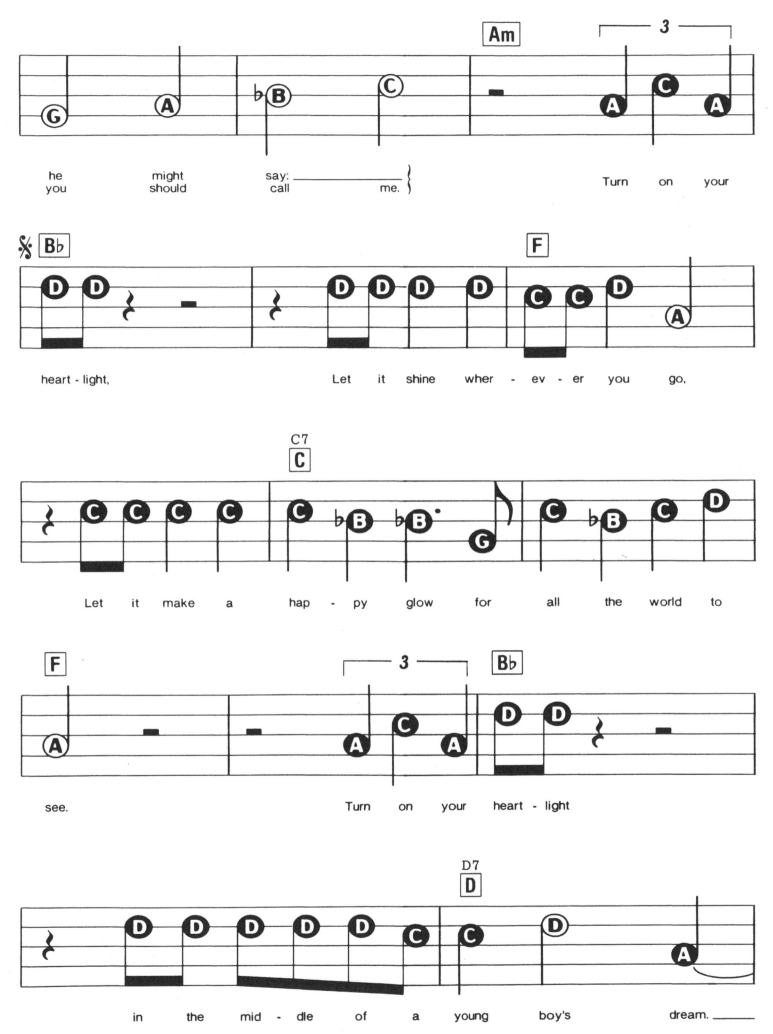

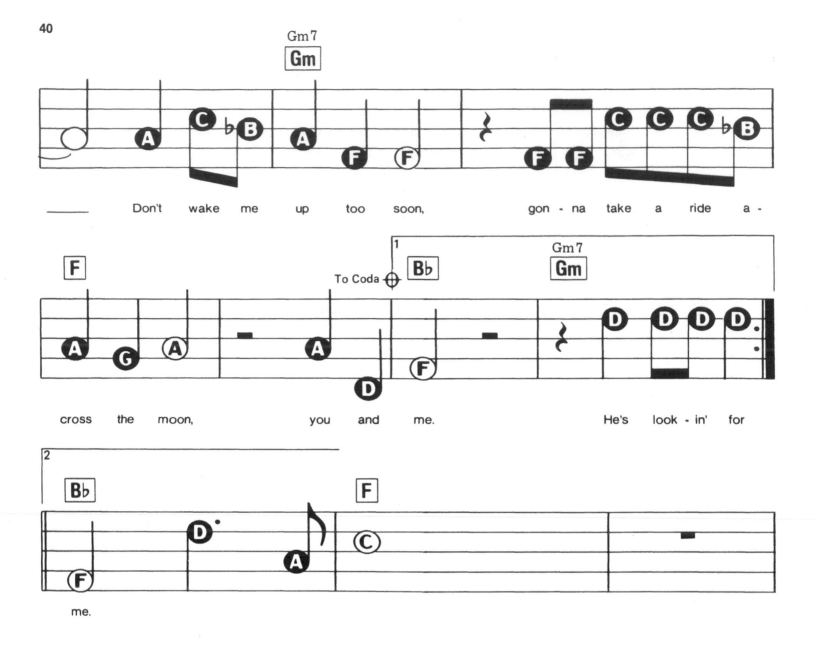

Don't wake me up too soon, gon - na take a ride a -

cross the moon, you and me. He's look - in' for

me.

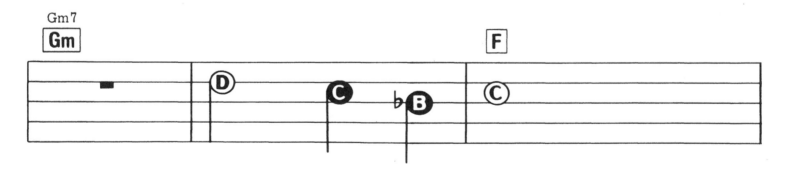

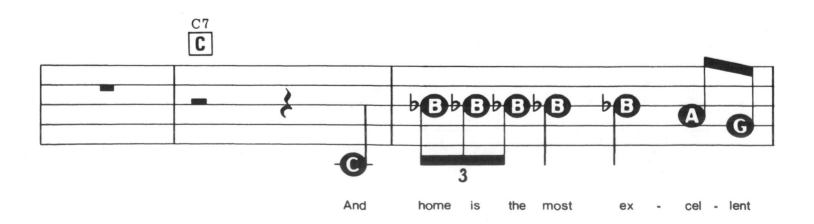

And home is the most ex - cel - lent

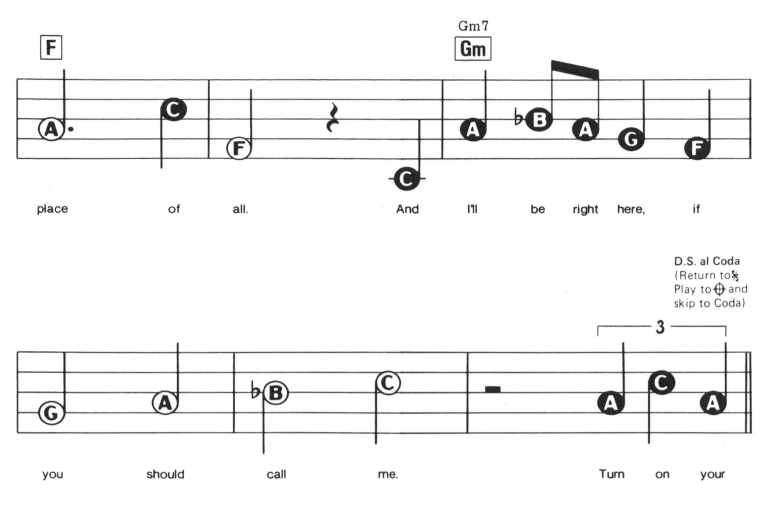

place   of   all.   And   I'll   be   right   here,   if

D.S. al Coda
(Return to 𝄋
Play to ⨁ and
skip to Coda)

⌐——— 3 ———⌐

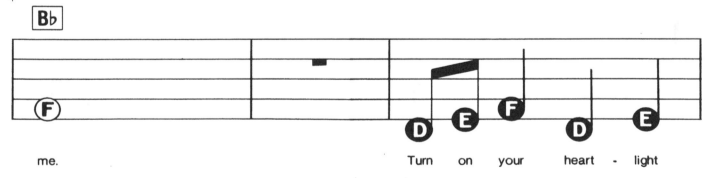

you   should   call   me.   Turn   on   your

⨁ CODA

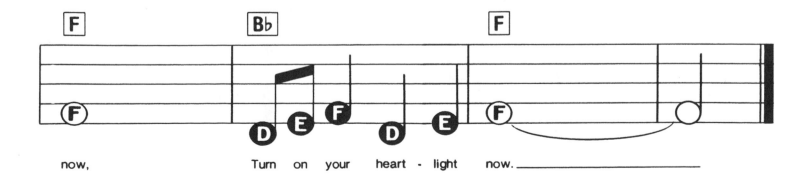

me.   Turn   on   your   heart - light

now,   Turn   on   your   heart - light   now._____

Do It

Registration 5
Rhythm: Rock

Words and Music by
Neil Diamond

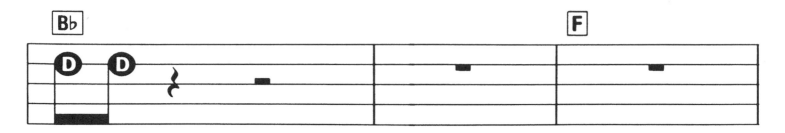

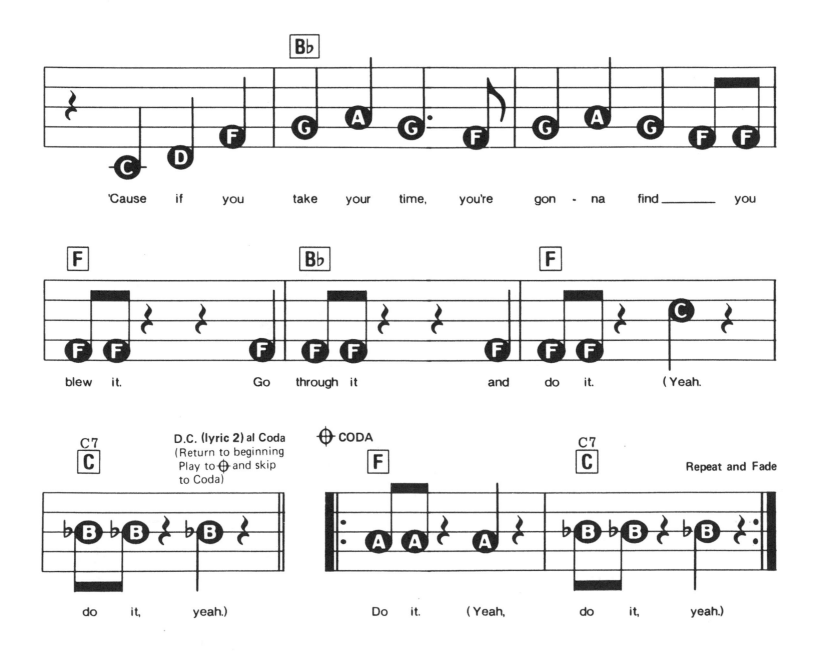

Forever In Blue Jeans

Registration 1
Rhythm: Fox Trot or Rock

Words and Music by
Neil Diamond and Richard Bennett

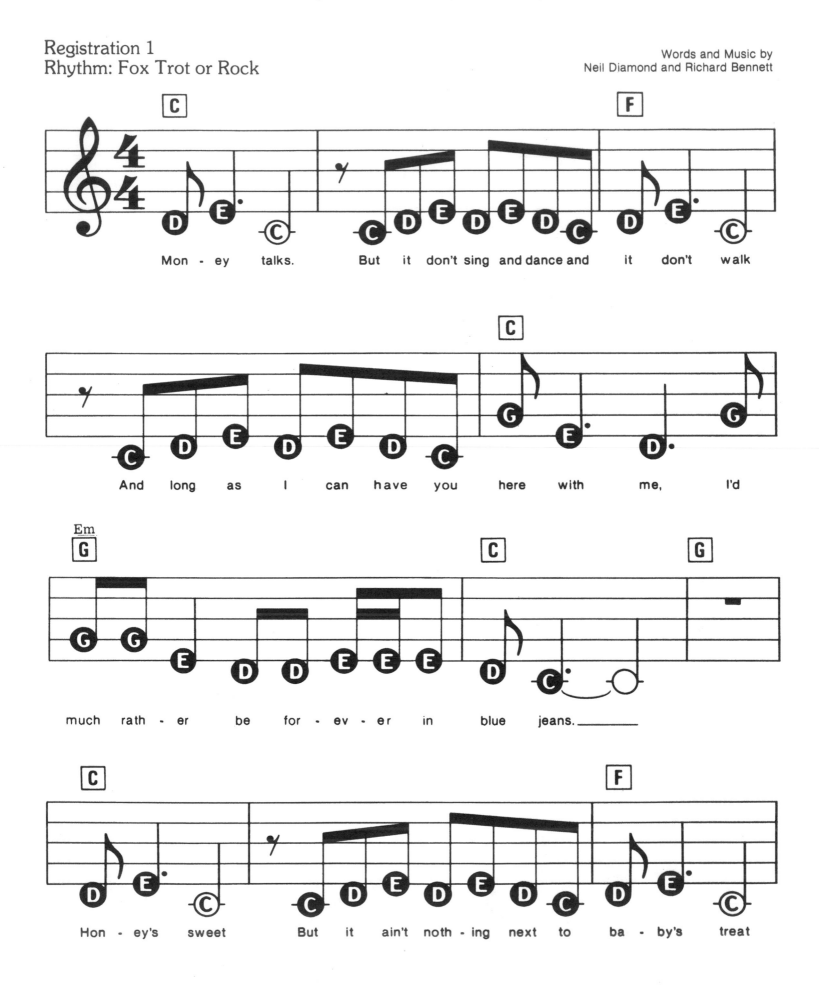

45

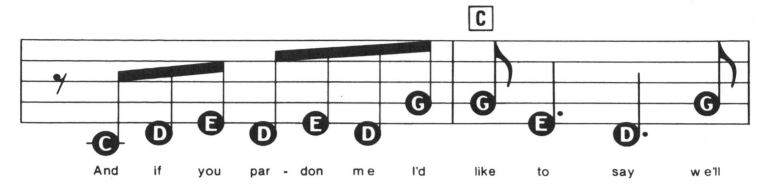

And if you par - don me I'd like to say we'll

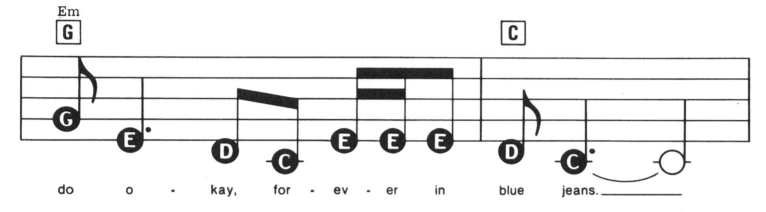

do o - kay, for - ev - er in blue jeans. _____

May - be to - nite. may - be to -

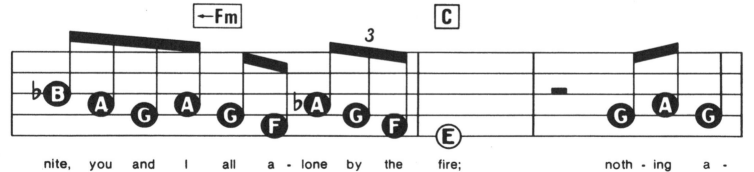

nite, you and I all a - lone by the fire; noth - ing a -

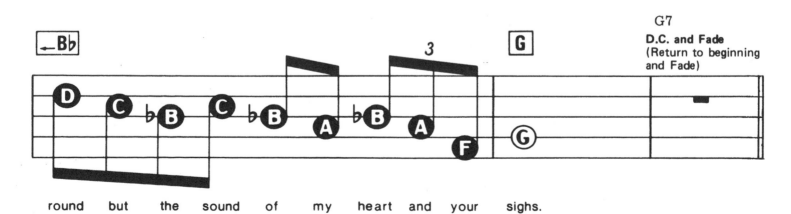

round but the sound of my heart and your sighs.

Front Page Story

Registration 4
Rhythm: Bossa Nova

Words and Music by Neil Diamond,
Burt Bacharach and Carole Bayer Sager

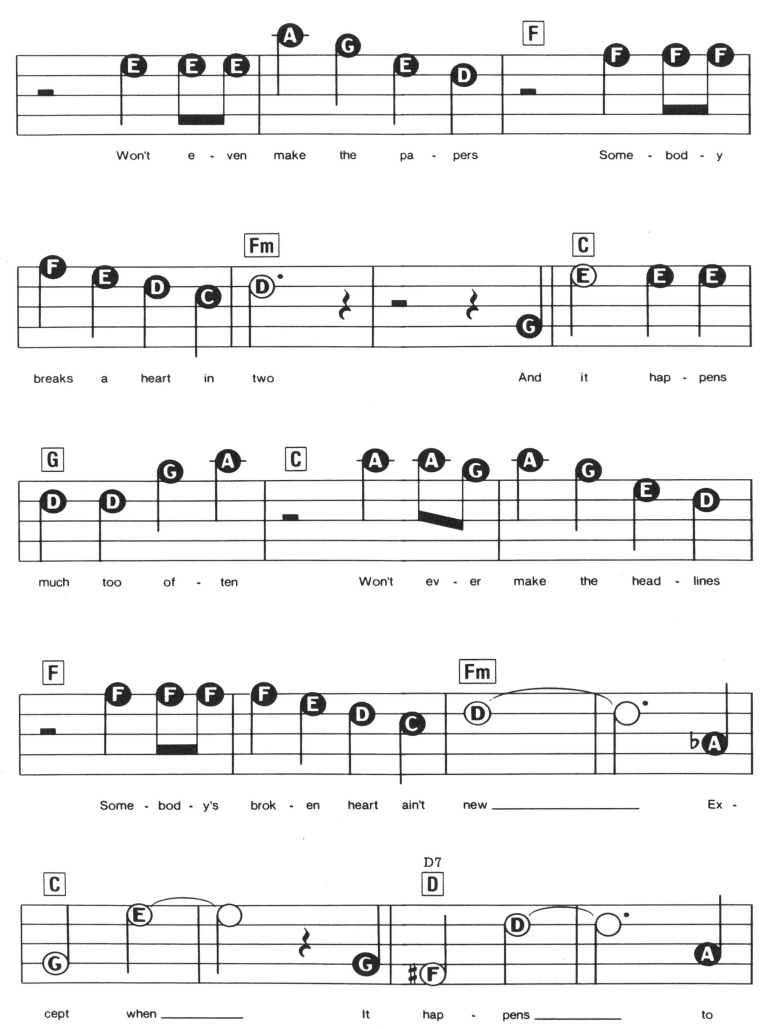

47

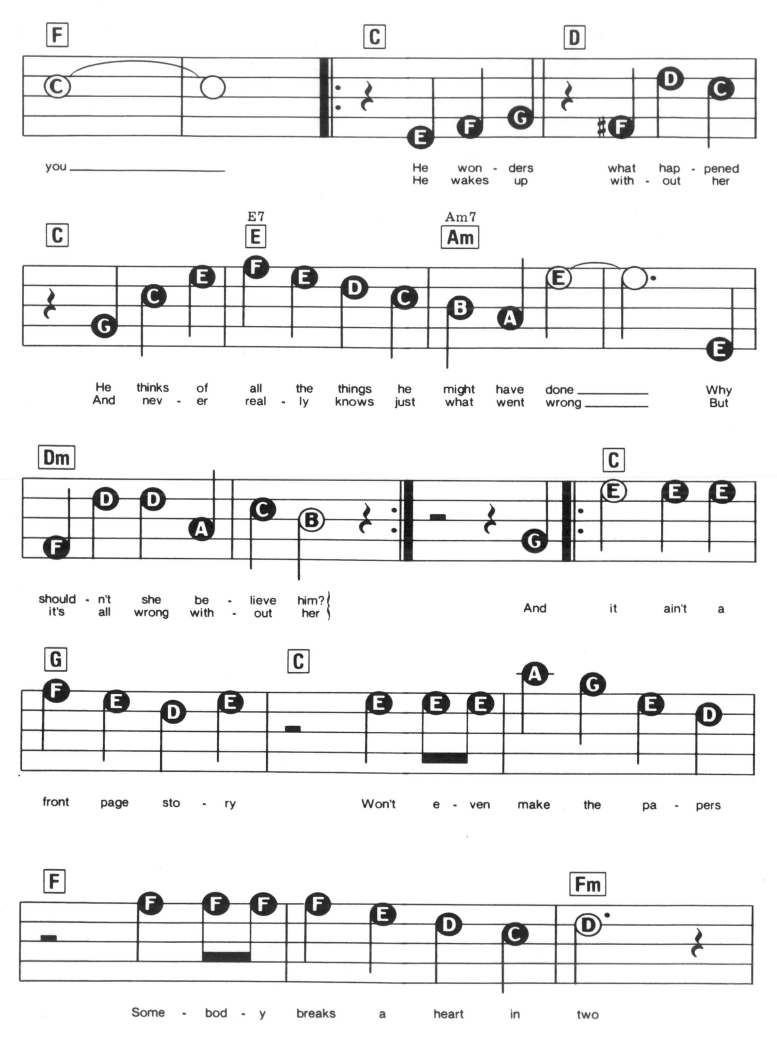

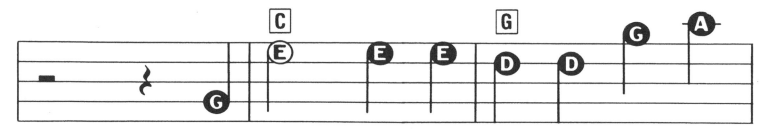

And it hap - pens much too of - ten

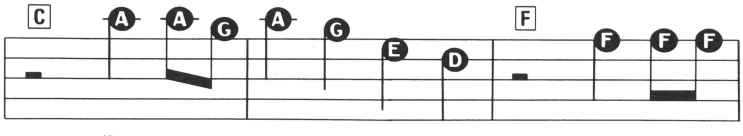

Won't ev - er make the head - lines An - oth - er

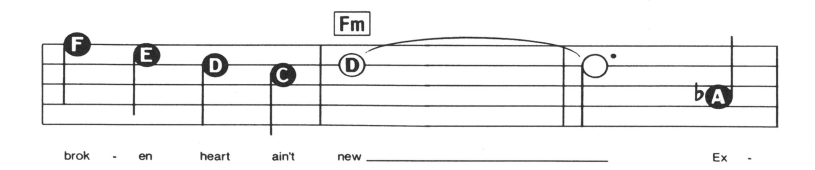

brok - en heart ain't new _____ Ex -

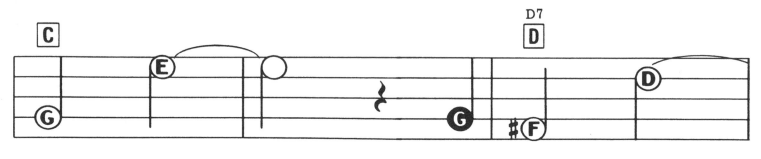

cept when _____ It hap - pens _____

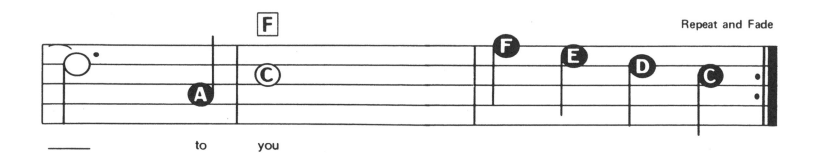

_____ to you

Girl, You'll Be A Woman Soon

Registration 3
Rhythm: Ballad or Fox Trot

Words and Music by
Neil Diamond

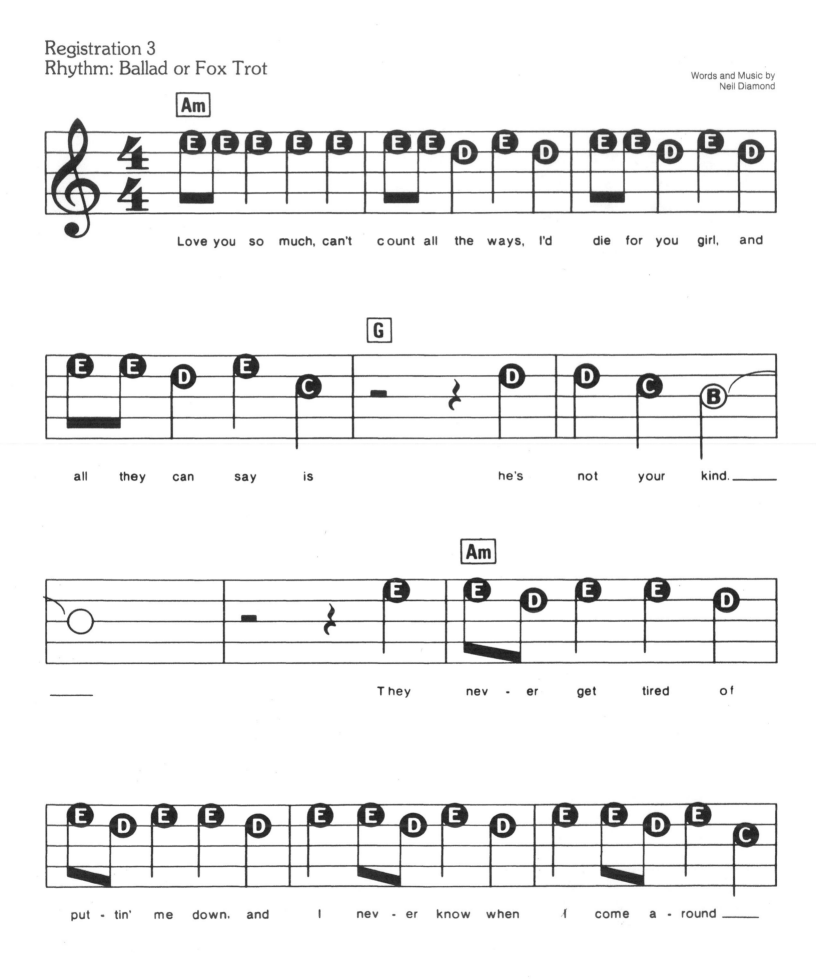

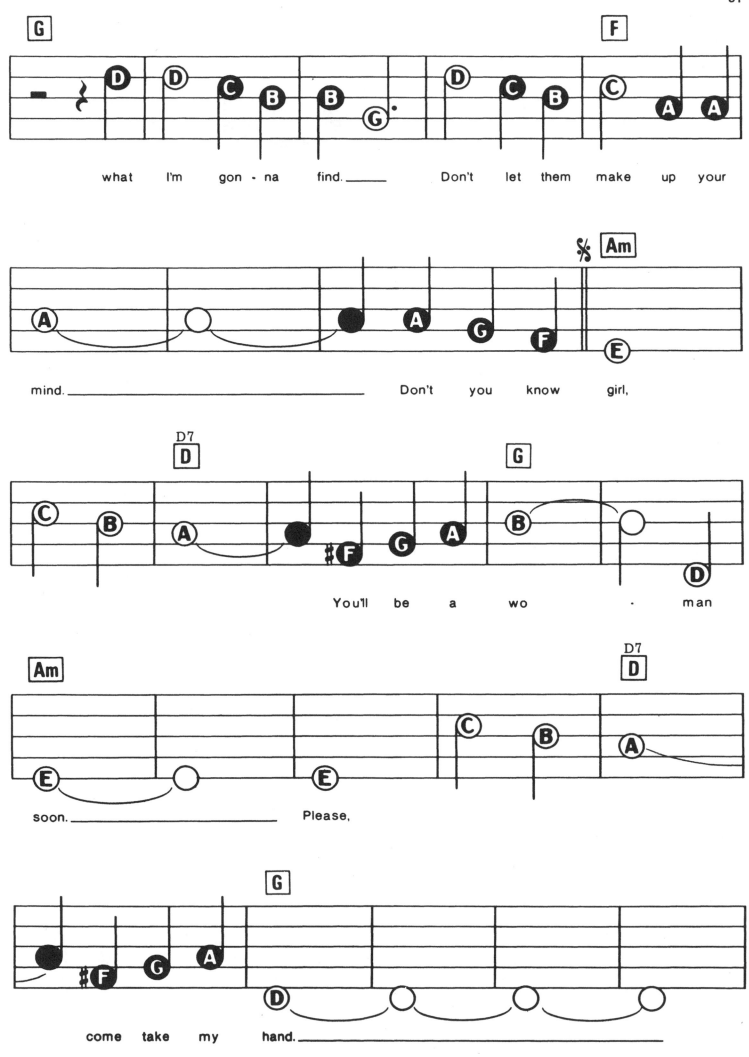

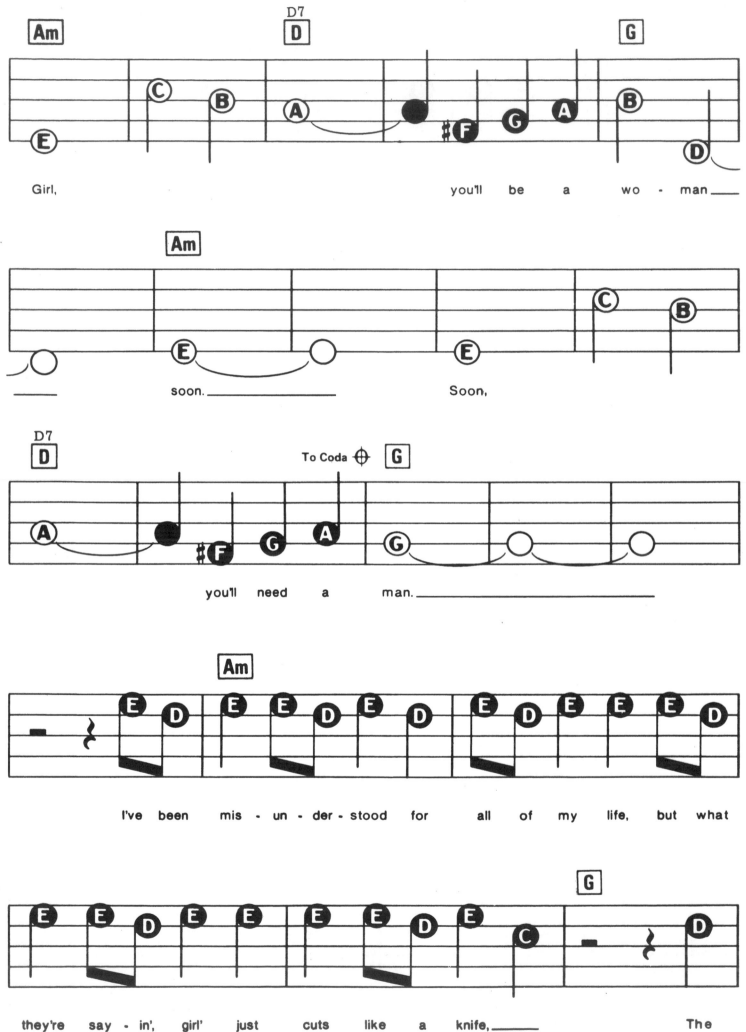

Girl, you'll be a wo - man ____

____ soon. ____ Soon,

you'll need a man. ____

I've been mis - un - der - stood for all of my life, but what

they're say - in', girl' just cuts like a knife, ____ The

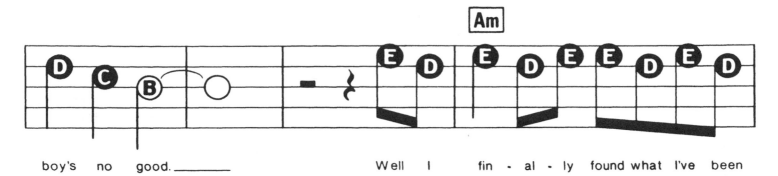

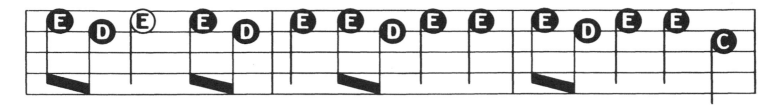

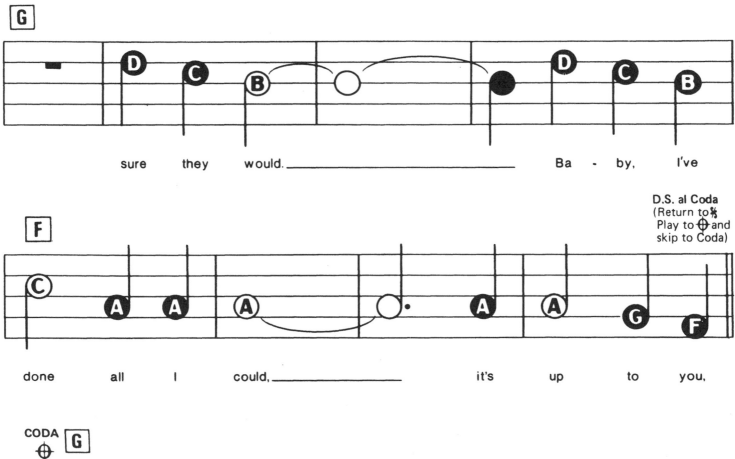

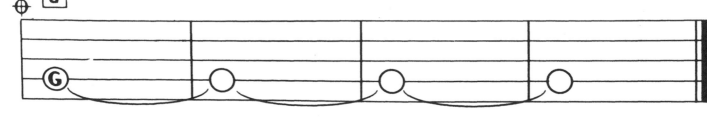

Havah Nagilah

From the Motion Picture "The Jazz Singer"

Registration 10

Traditional
Adaptation by Neil Diamond

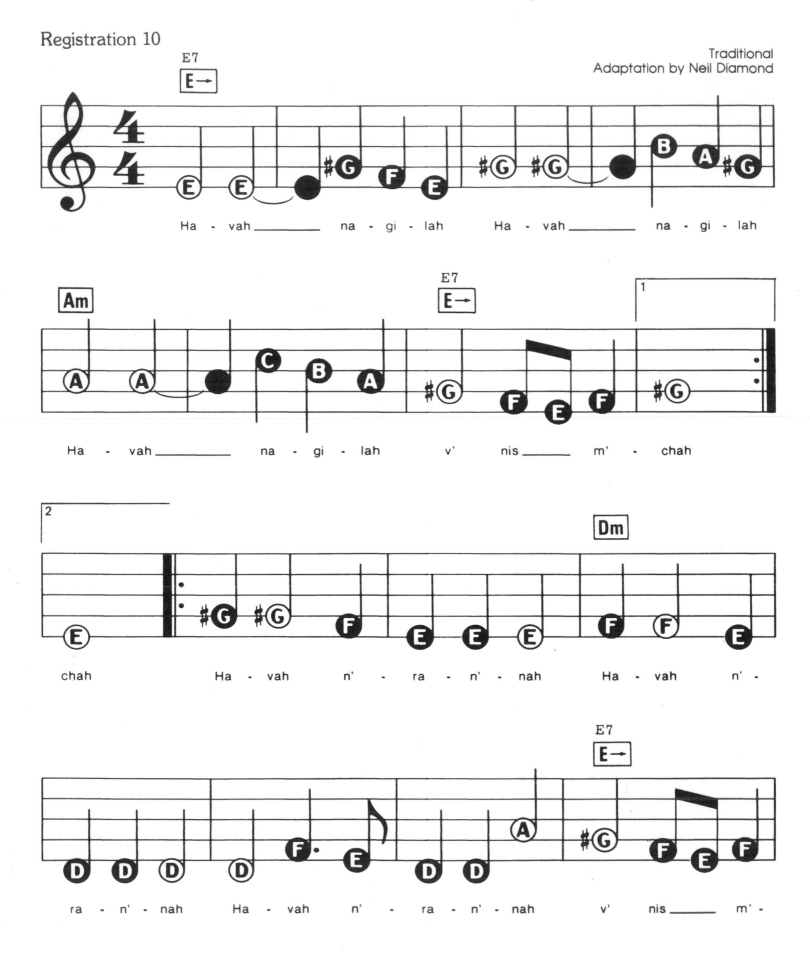

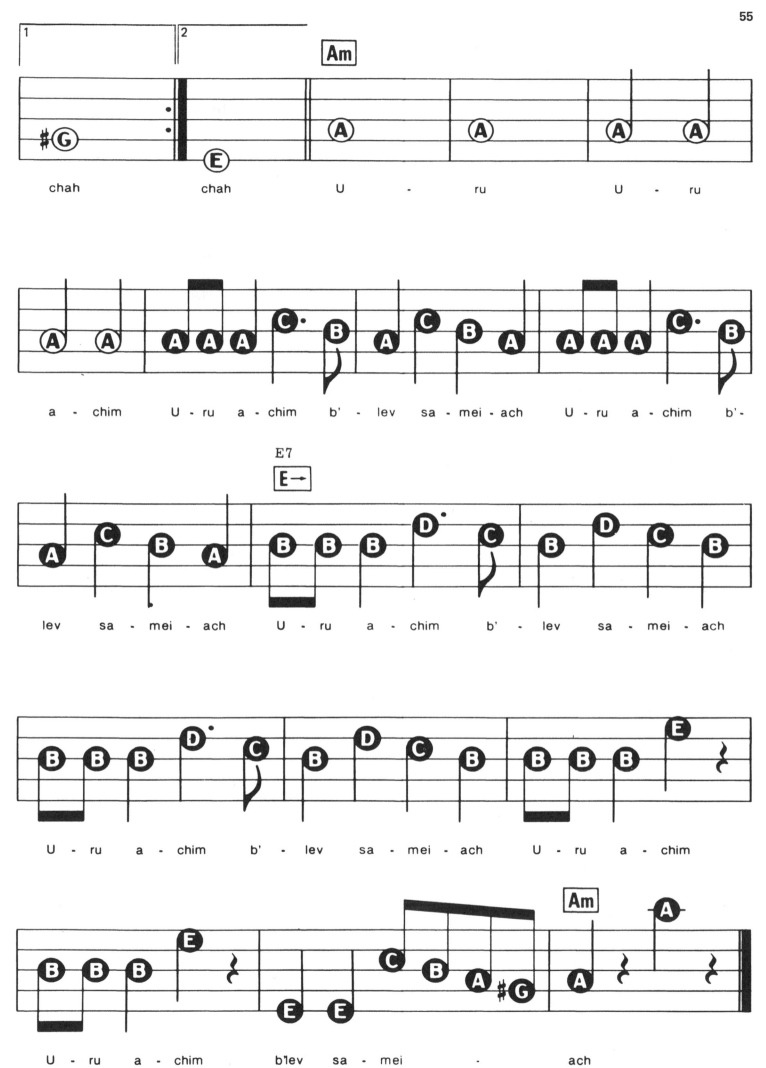

Hello Again

From the Motion Picture "The Jazz Singer"

Words by Neil Diamond
Music by Neil Diamond and Alan Lindgren

Registration 1
Rhythm: Rock or Fox Trot

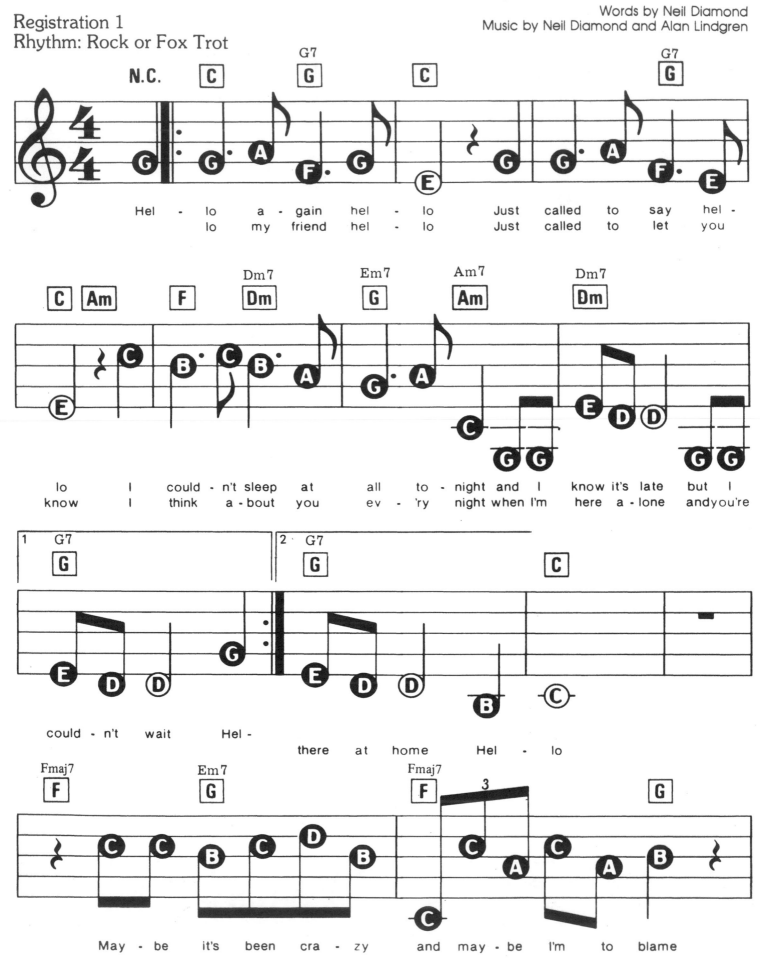

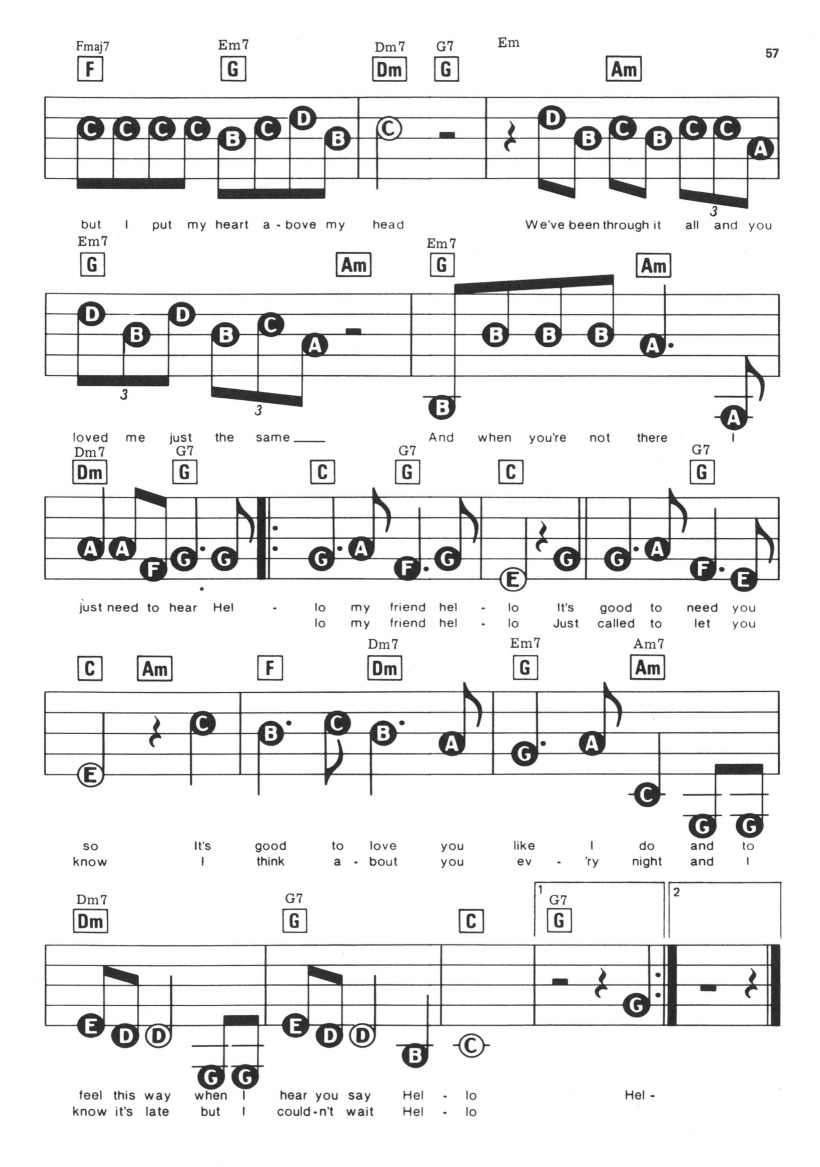

Holly Holy

Registration 2
Rhythm: Ballad or Fox Trot

Words and Music by
Neil Diamond

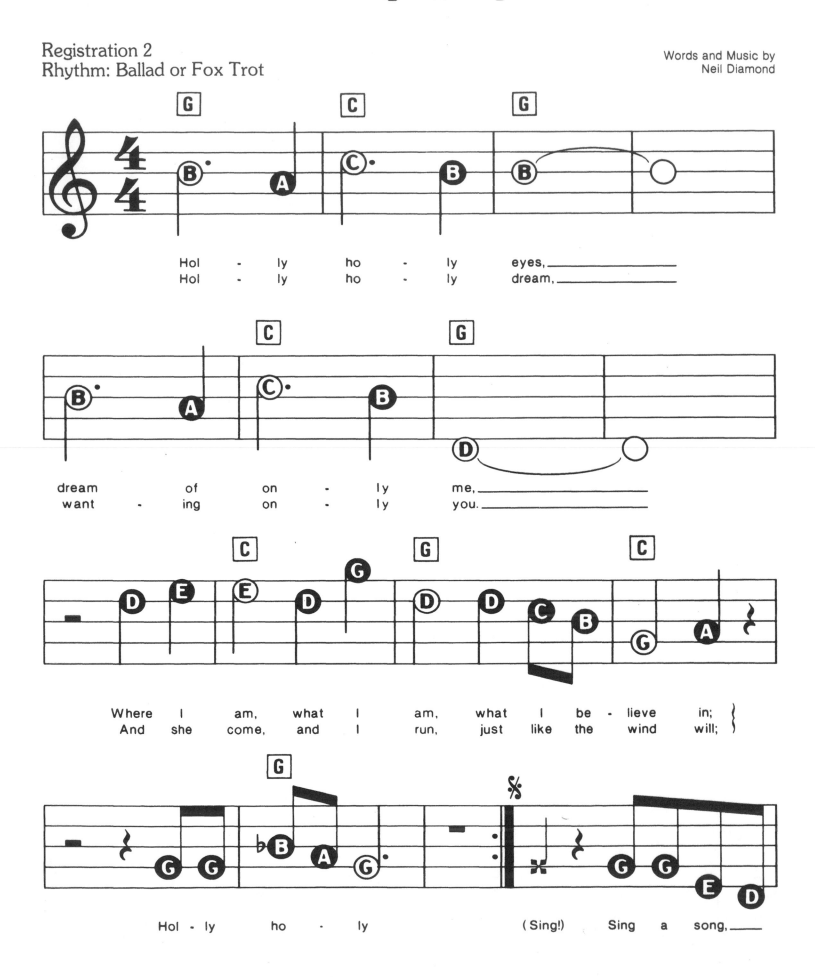

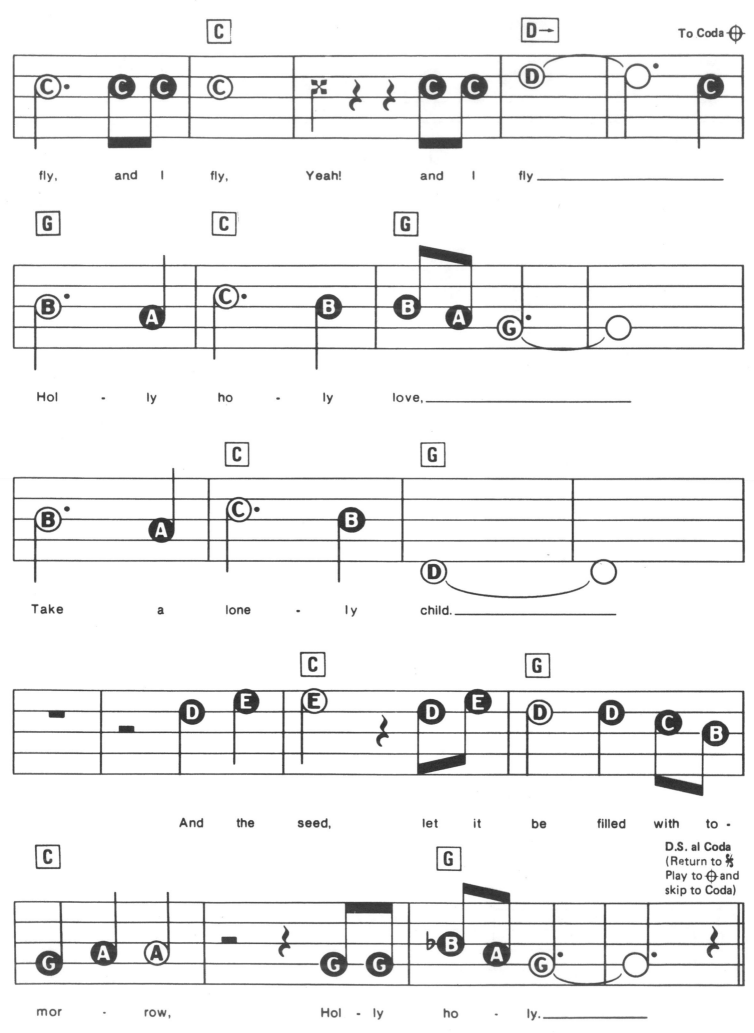

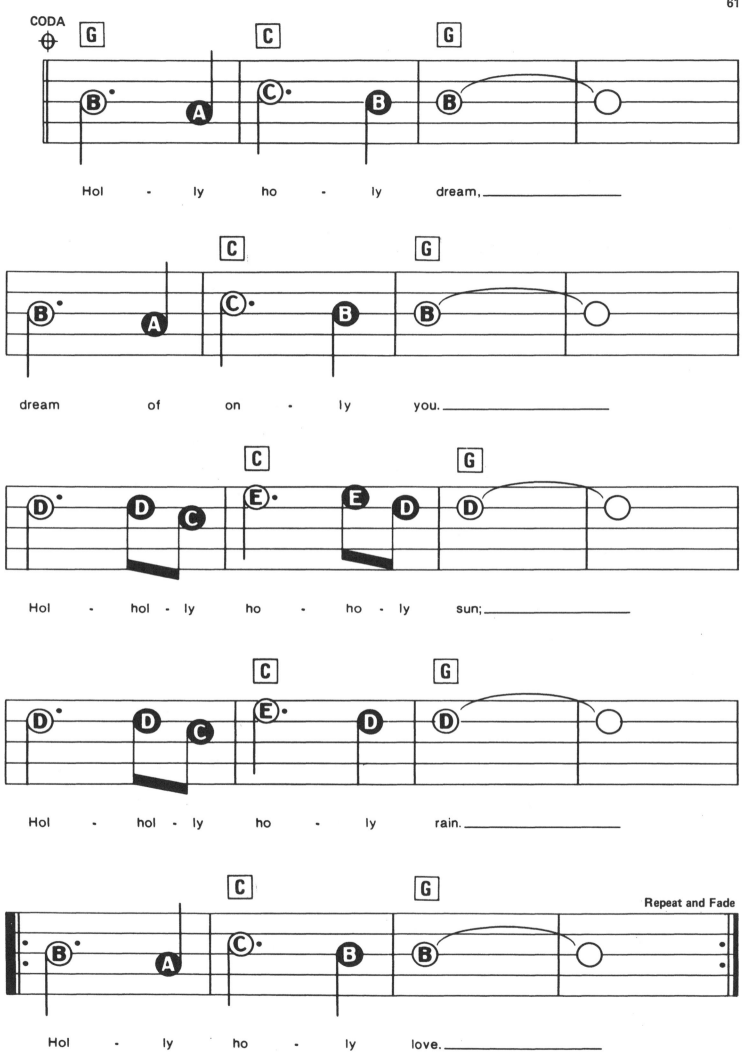

I Am...I Said

Registration 3
Rhythm: Fox Trot or March(4/4)

Words and Music by
Neil Diamond

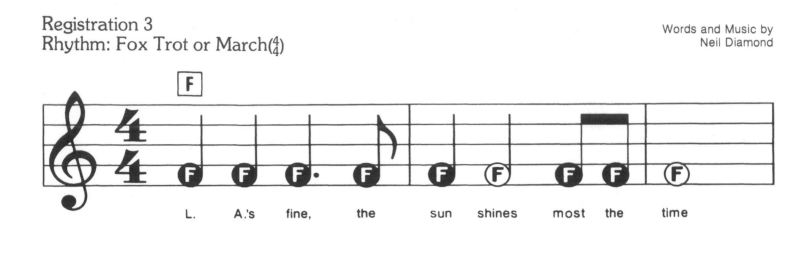

L. A.'s fine, the sun shines most the time

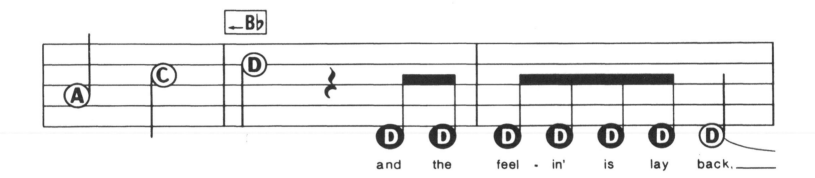

and the feel - in' is lay back, _____

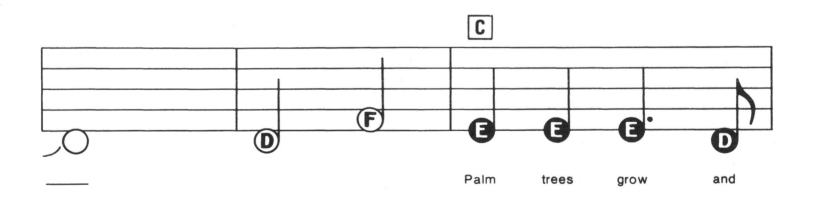

_____ Palm trees grow and

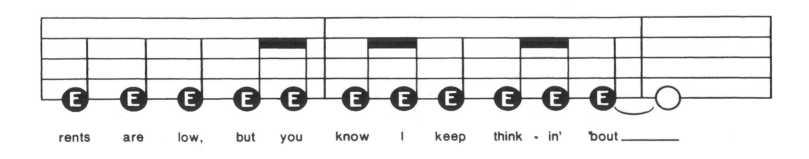

rents are low, but you know I keep think - in' 'bout _____

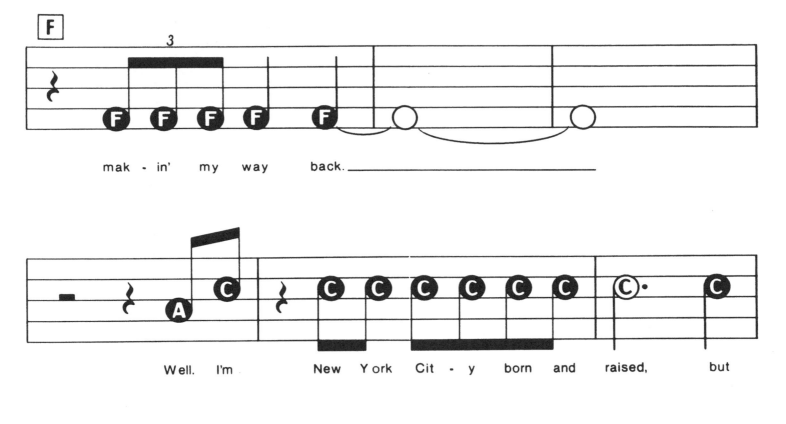

mak - in' my way back.

Well. I'm New York Cit - y born and raised, but

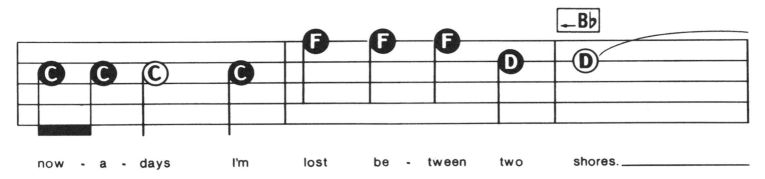

now - a - days I'm lost be - tween two shores.

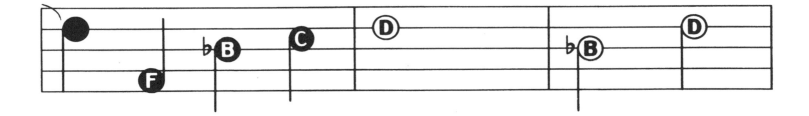

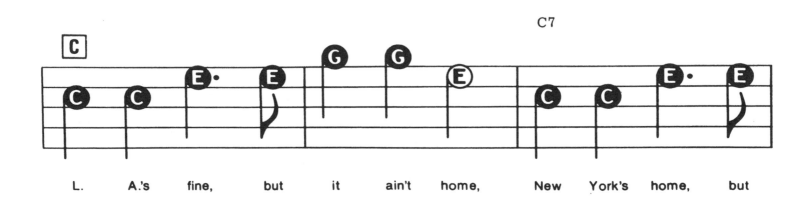

L. A.'s fine, but it ain't home, New York's home, but

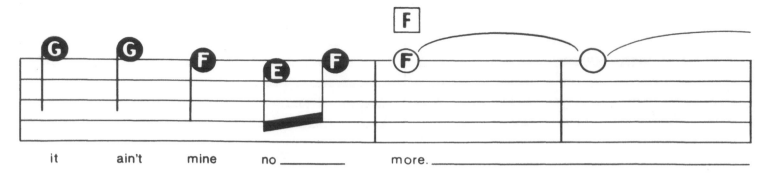

it   ain't   mine   no _____ more. _____

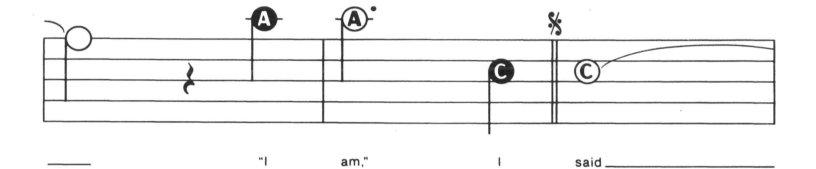

____   "I   am,"   I   said _____

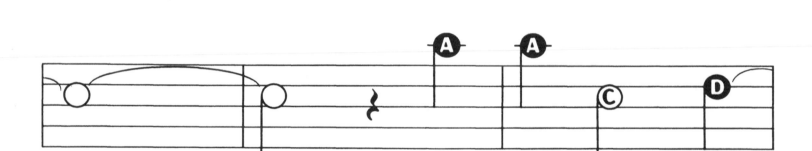

_____   to   no   one   there. ____

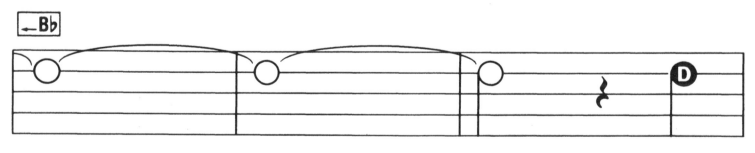

_____   And

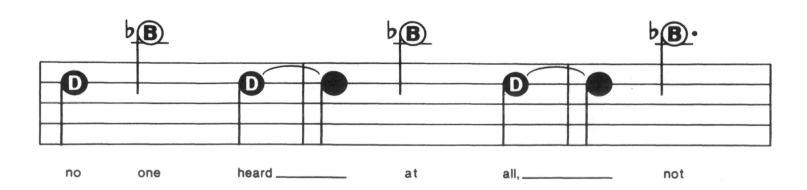

no   one   heard _____ at   all, _____ not

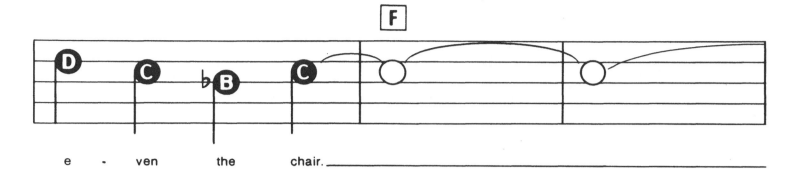

e - ven the chair._____

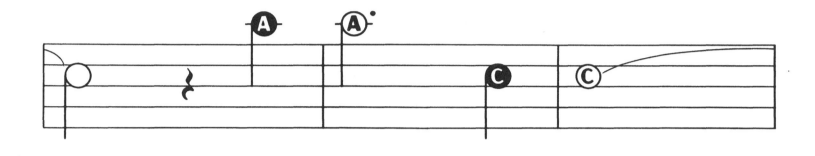

_____ "I am," I cried_____

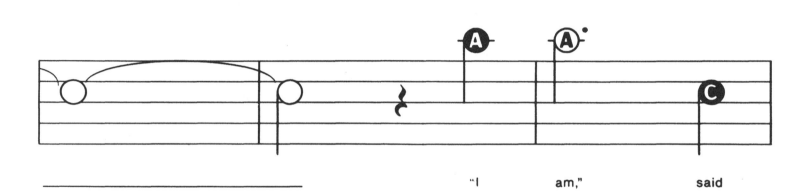

_____ "I am," said

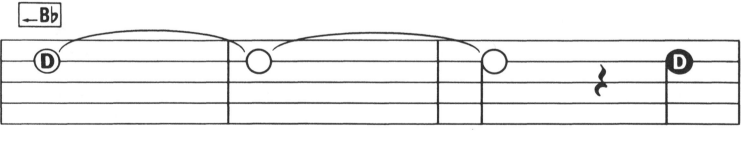

I,_____ and

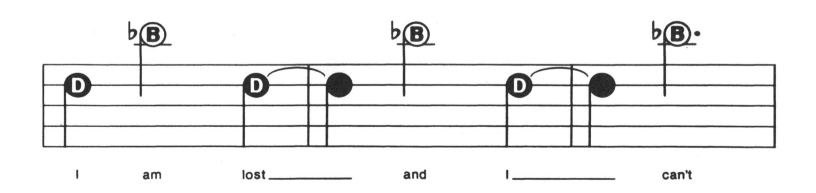

I am lost_____ and I_____ can't

66

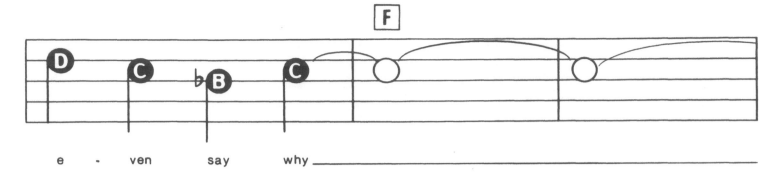

e - ven say why _____

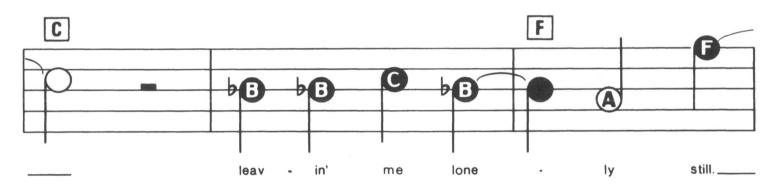

____ leav - in' me lone - ly still. ____

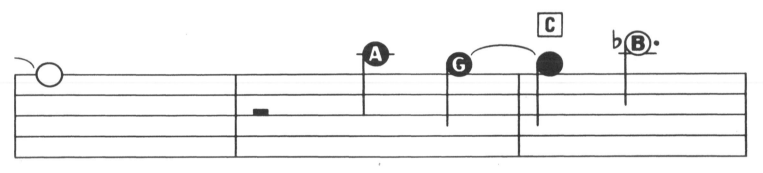

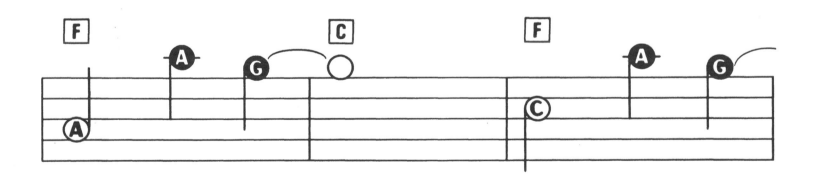

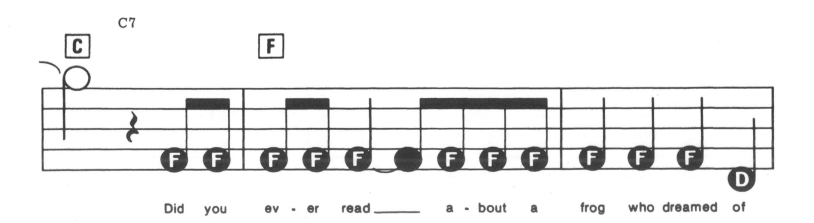

C7

Did you ev - er read ____ a - bout a frog who dreamed of

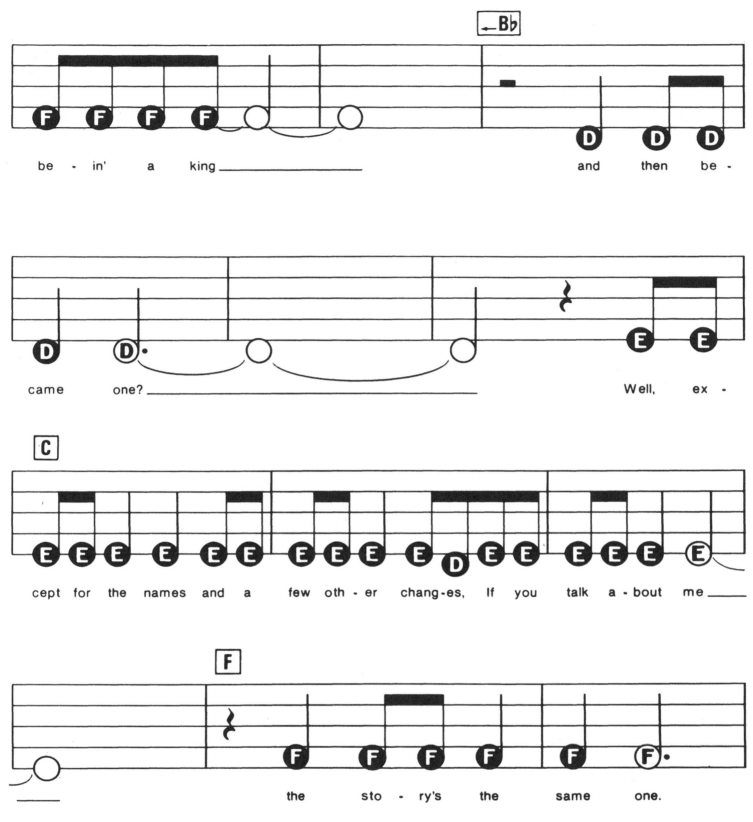

be - in' a king_____ and then be -

came one?_____ Well, ex -

cept for the names and a few oth - er chang-es, If you talk a - bout me____

the sto - ry's the same one.

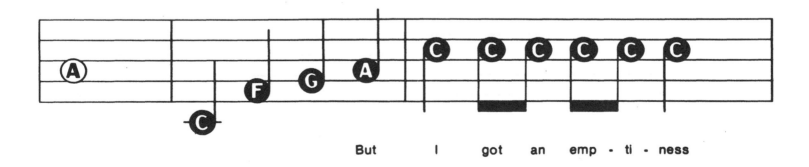

But I got an emp - ti - ness

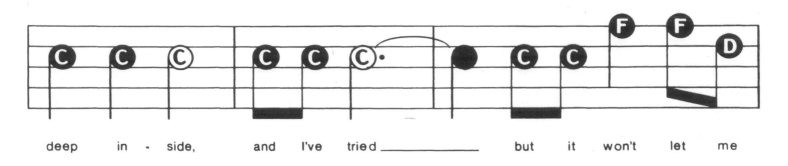

deep   in - side,   and   I've   tried _____   but   it   won't   let   me

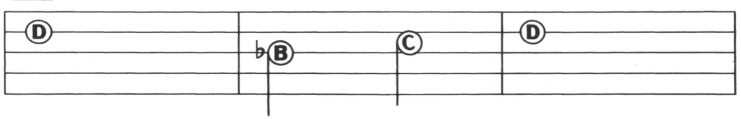

go.

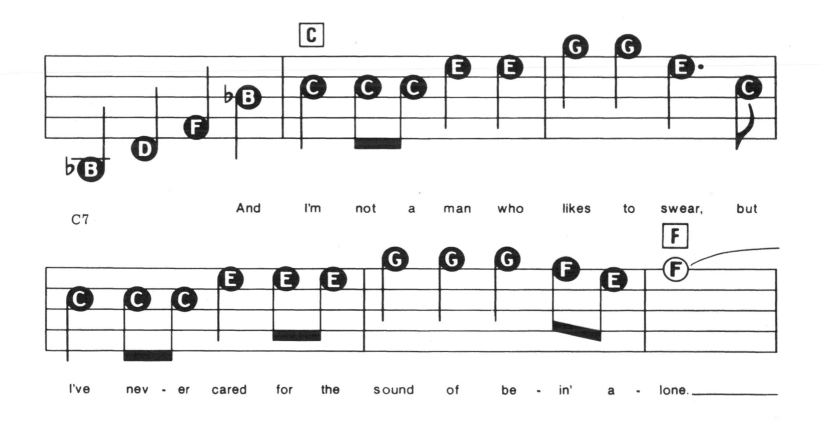

C7

And   I'm   not   a   man   who   likes   to   swear,   but

I've   nev - er   cared   for   the   sound   of   be - in'   a - lone._____

D.S. and Fade
(Return to ⅗ and Fade)

_____   "I   am,"   I

If You Know What I Mean

Registration 9
Rhythm: Rock or Jazz Rock

Words and Music by Neil Diamond

When the night re - turns just like a friend,

When the eve - ning comes to set me free, When the qui - et hours that wait be-

yond the day make peace - ful sounds in me;

Took a drag from my last cig - a - rette, Took a drink from a glass of old _____

wine, I closed my eyes and I could make it real and feel it one more

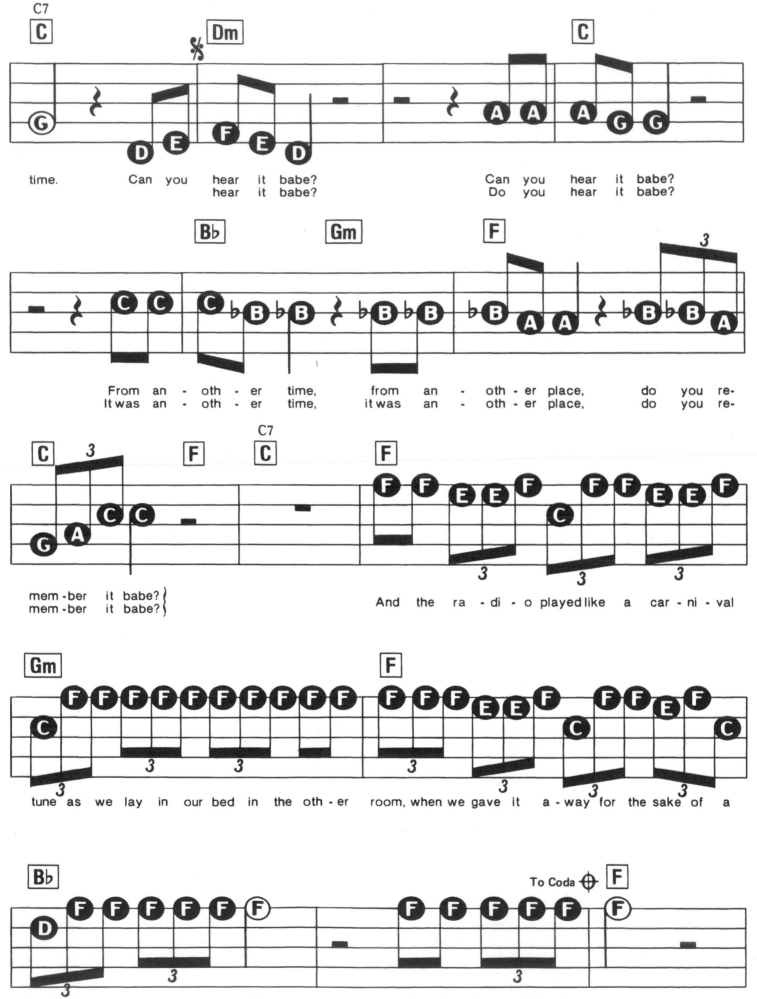

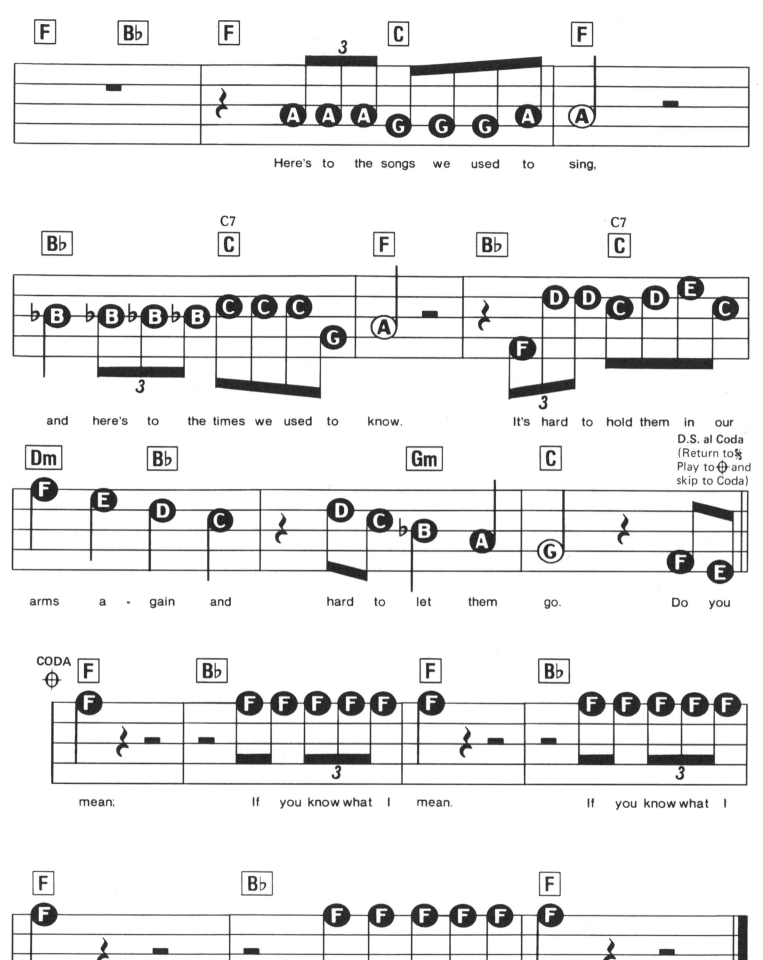

Here's to the songs we used to sing,

and here's to the times we used to know. It's hard to hold them in our

D.S. al Coda
(Return to %
Play to ⊕ and
skip to Coda)

arms a - gain and hard to let them go. Do you

CODA

mean; If you know what I mean. If you know what I

mean; if you know what I mean.

If I Never Knew Your Name

Registration 1
Rhythm: Ballad or Fox Trot

Words and Music by
Neil Diamond

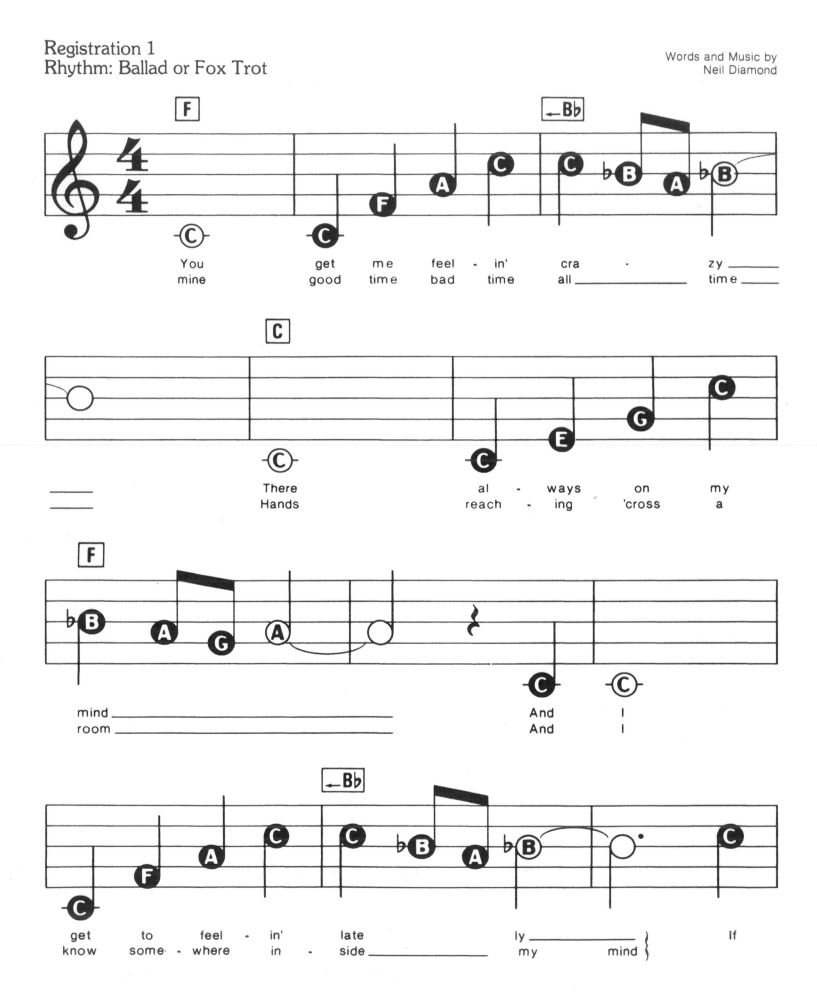

73

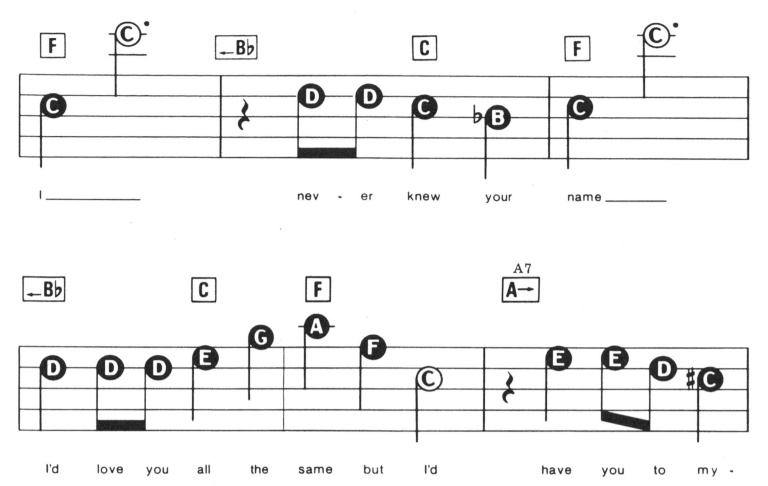

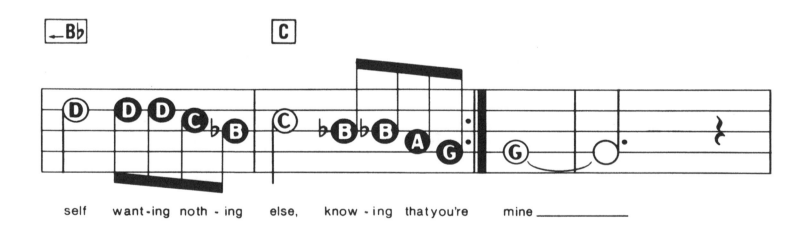

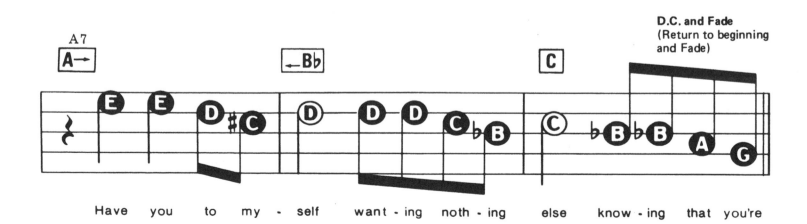

I'm A Believer

Registration 5
Rhythm: Rock

Words and Music by
Neil Diamond

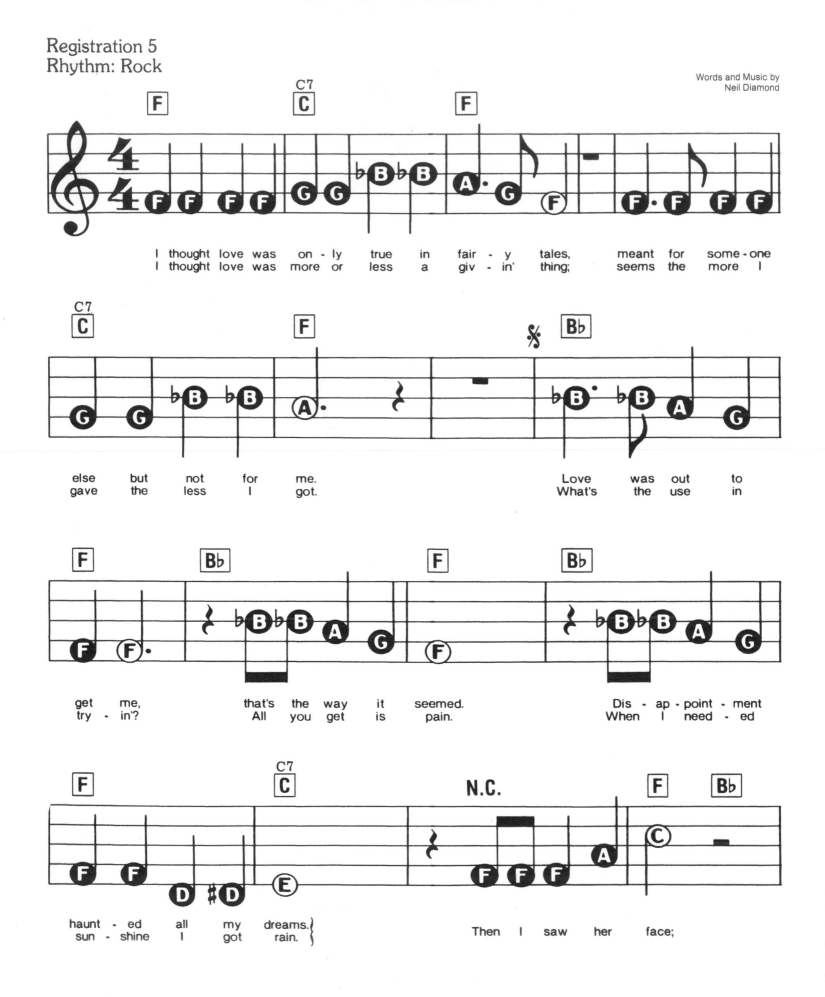

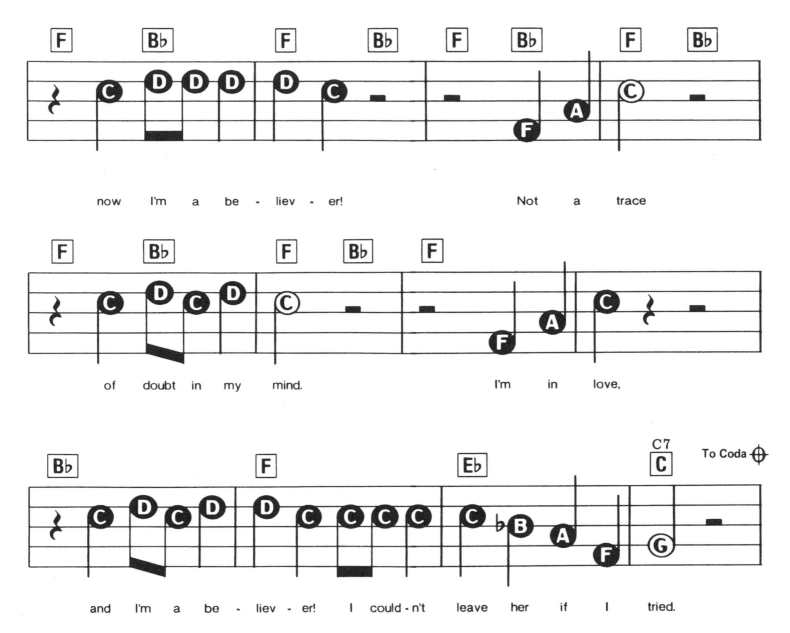

now I'm a be - liev - er! Not a trace

of doubt in my mind. I'm in love,

and I'm a be - liev - er! I could-n't leave her if I tried.

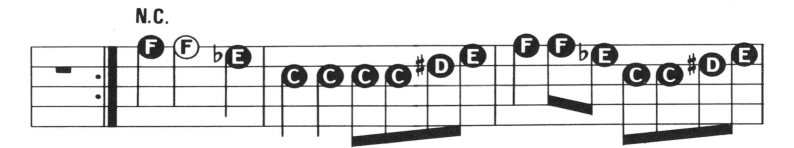

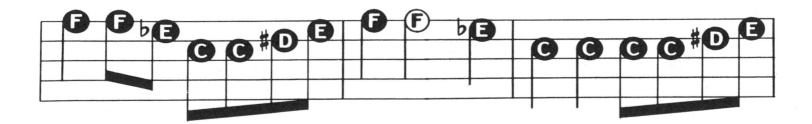

Jerusalem

From the Motion Picture "The Jazz Singer"

Registration 8
Rhythm: Latin or Rock

Words and Music by
Neil Diamond

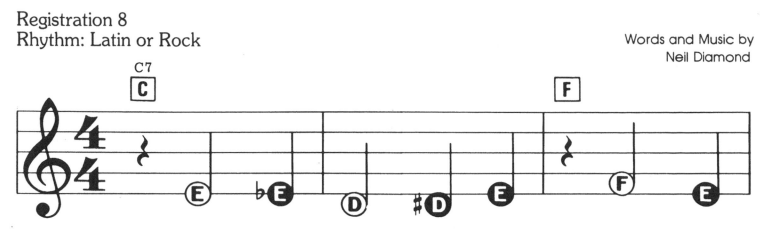

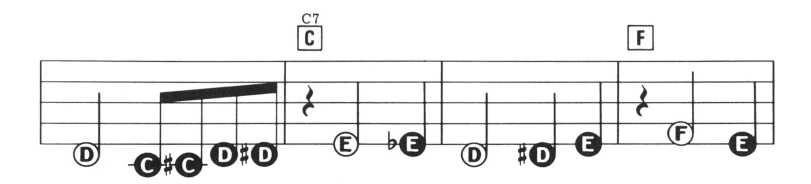

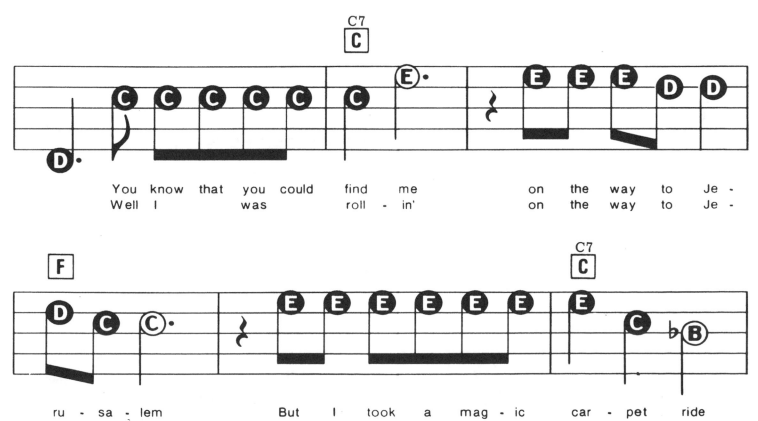

You know that you could find me   on the way to Je -
Well I   was   roll - in'   on the way to Je -

ru - sa - lem   But I took a mag - ic car - pet ride
ru - sa - lem   I was head - ed for the prom - ised land

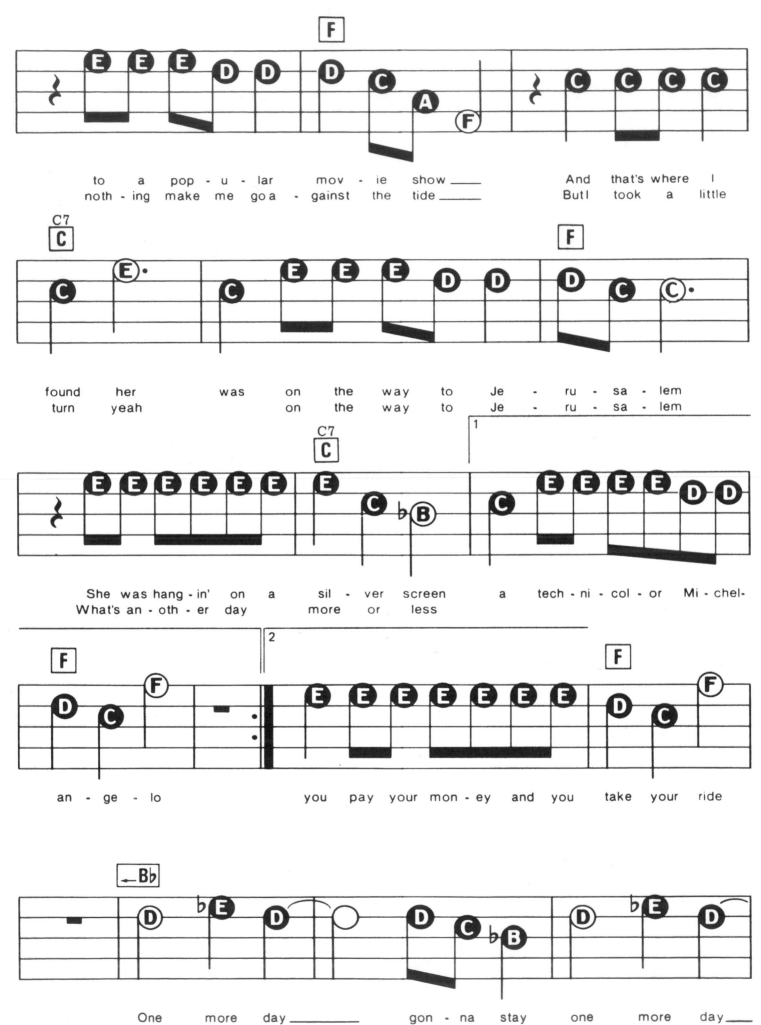

to a pop - u - lar mov - ie show ____ And that's where I
noth - ing make me go a - gainst the tide ____ But I took a little

found her was on the way to Je - ru - sa - lem
turn yeah on the way to Je - ru - sa - lem

She was hang - in' on a sil - ver screen a tech - ni - col - or Mi - chel -
What's an - oth - er day more or less

an - ge - lo you pay your mon - ey and you take your ride

One more day ____ gon - na stay one more day ____

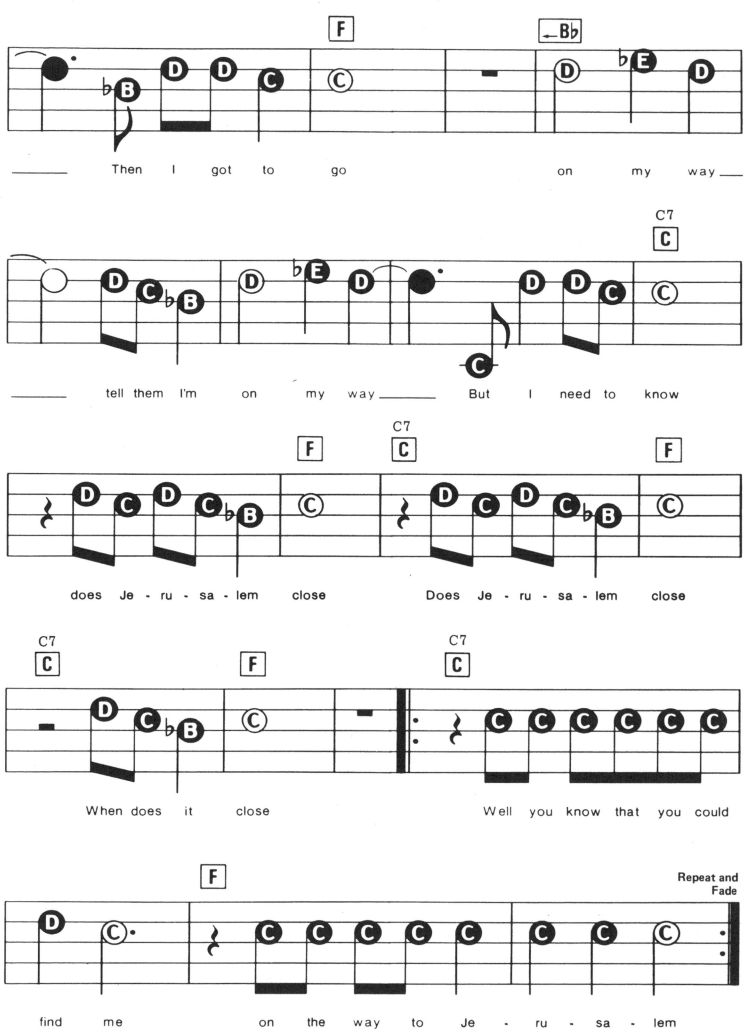

I'm Alive

Registration 8
Rhythm: Rock

Words and Music by Neil Diamond
and David Foster

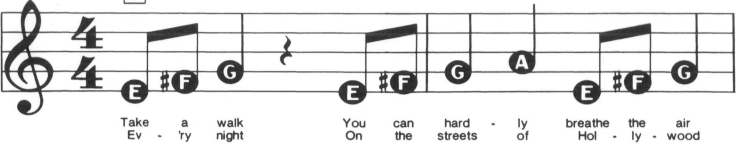

Take a walk
Ev - 'ry night
You can hard - ly
On the streets of
breathe the air
Hol - ly - wood

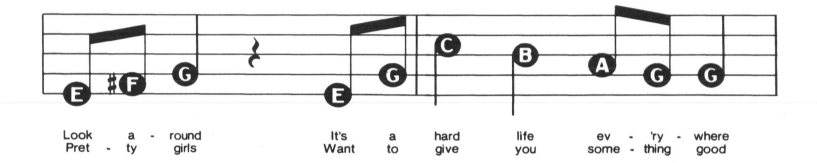

Look a - round
Pret - ty girls
It's a hard life
Want to give you
ev - 'ry - where
some - thing good

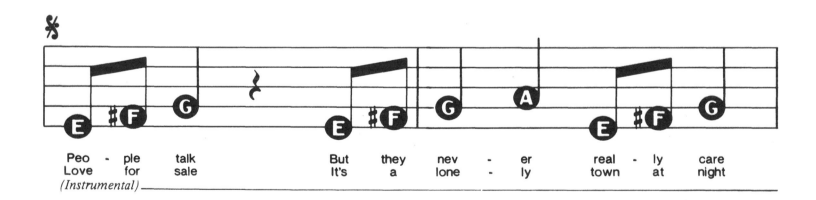

Peo - ple talk
Love for sale
But they nev - er
It's a lone - ly
real - ly care
town at night

(Instrumental) _____

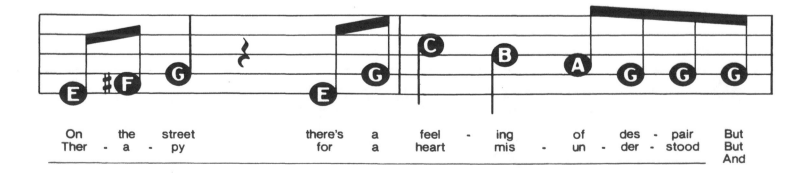

On the street
Ther - a - py
there's a feel - ing
for a heart mis -
of des - pair
un - der - stood
But
But
And

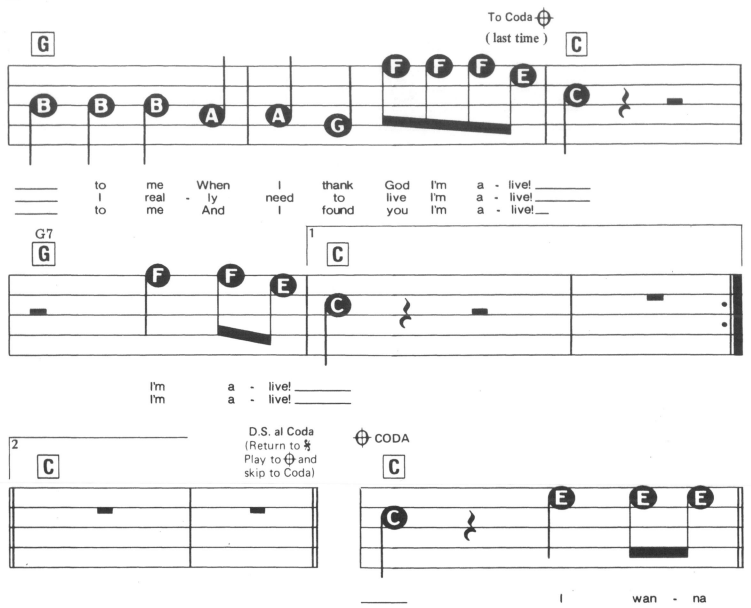

to me   When   I   thank   God   I'm   a - live! _____
I   real - ly   need   to   live   I'm   a - live! _____
to me   And   I   found   you   I'm   a - live! __

I'm   a - live! _____
I'm   a - live! _____

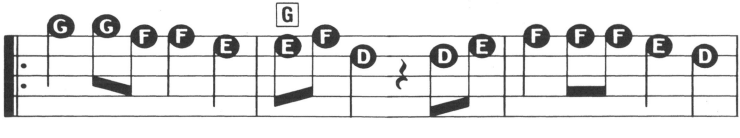

_____   I   wan - na

take   all   that   life   has   got   to   give   All   I   need   is   some - one   to

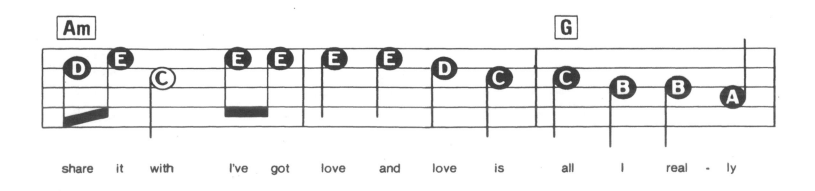

share   it   with   I've   got   love   and   love   is   all   I   real - ly

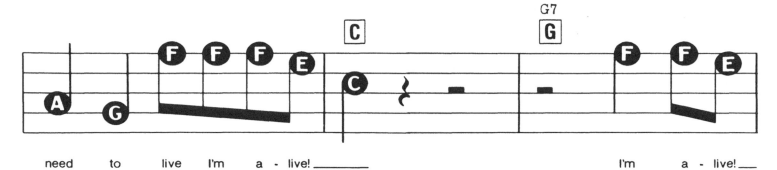

need to live I'm a - live! _____ I'm a - live! ___

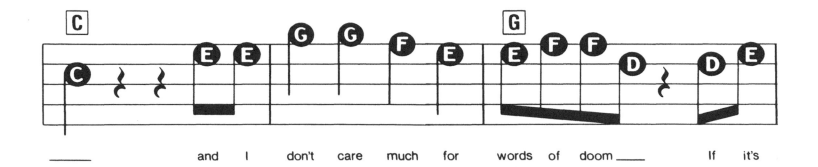

_____ and I don't care much for words of doom ____ If it's

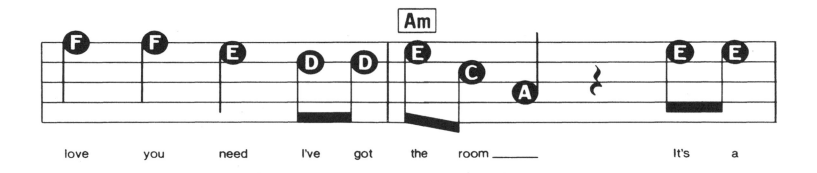

love you need I've got the room _____ It's a

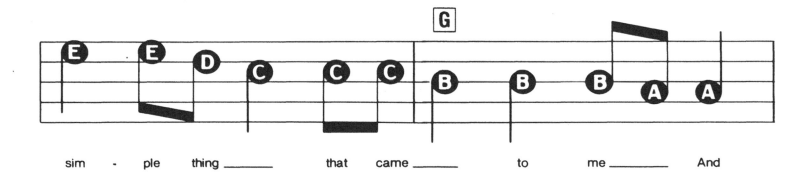

sim - ple thing _____ that came _____ to me _____ And

Repeat and Fade

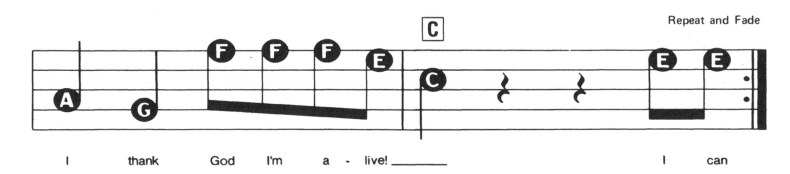

I thank God I'm a - live! _____ I can

Kentucky Woman

Registration 4
Rhythm: Fox Trot or Slow Rock

Words and Music by
Neil Diamond

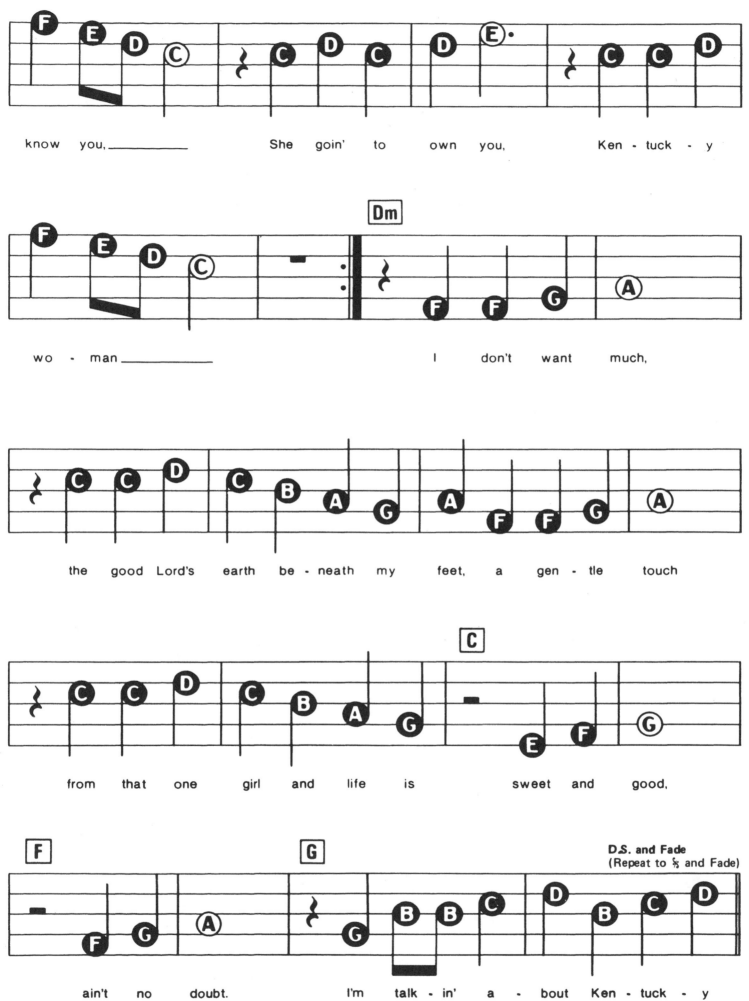

Let The Little Boy Sing

Registration 6
Rhythm: Rock or Jazz Rock

Words and Music by Neil Diamond
and Bob Gaudio

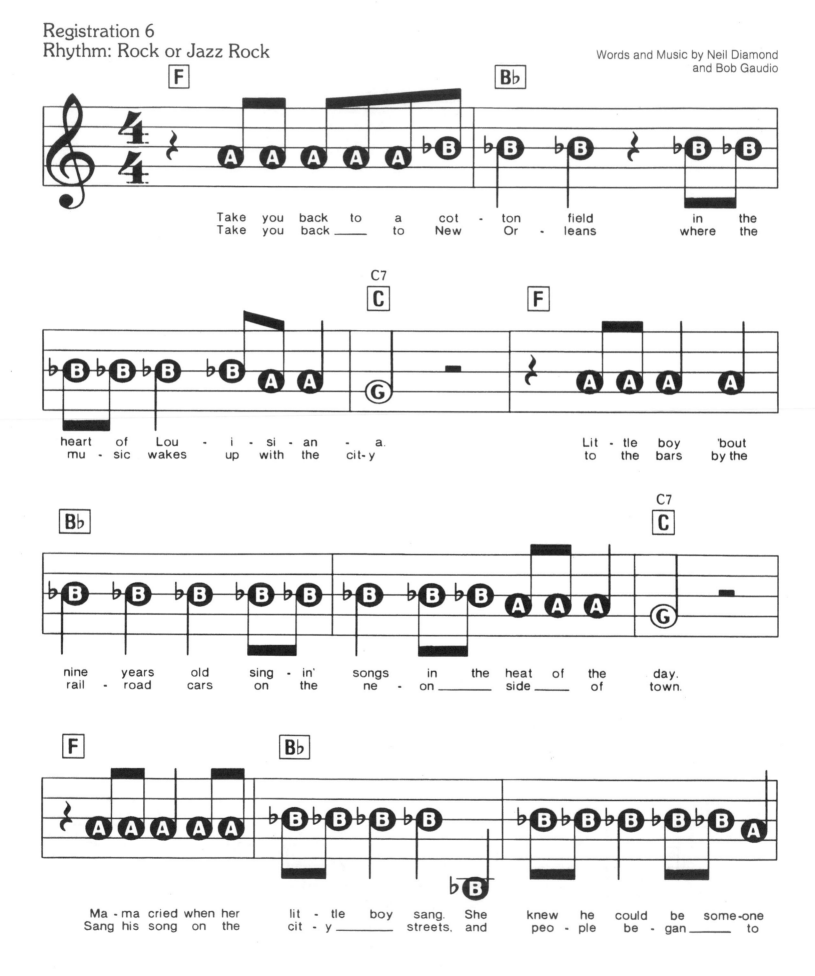

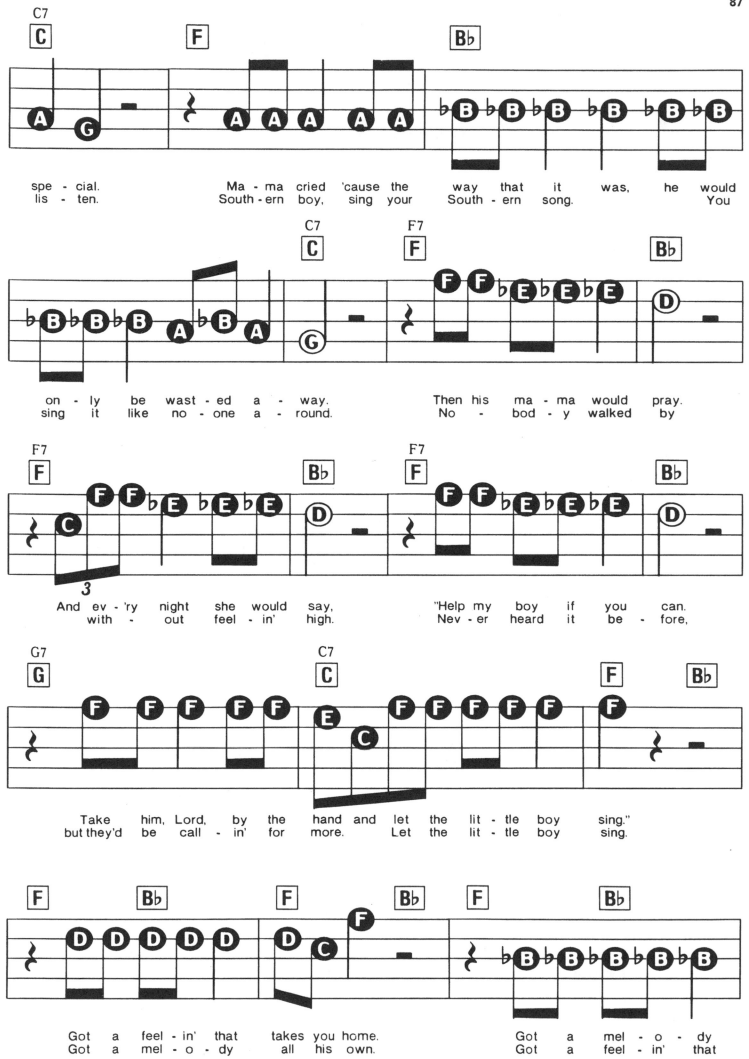

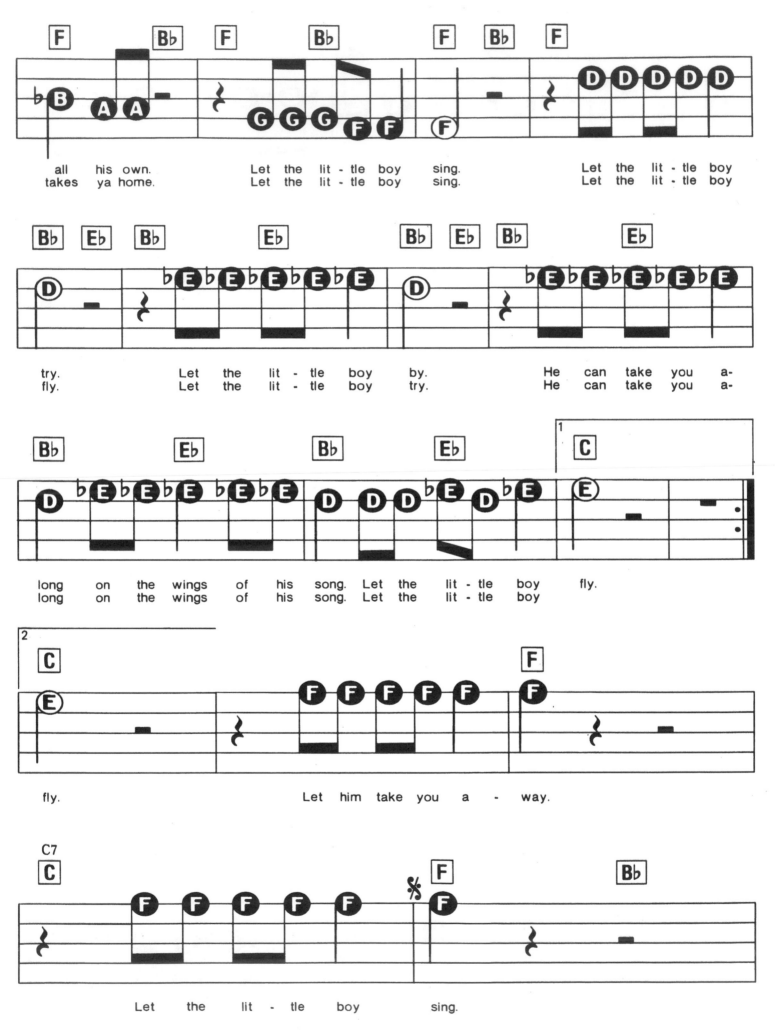

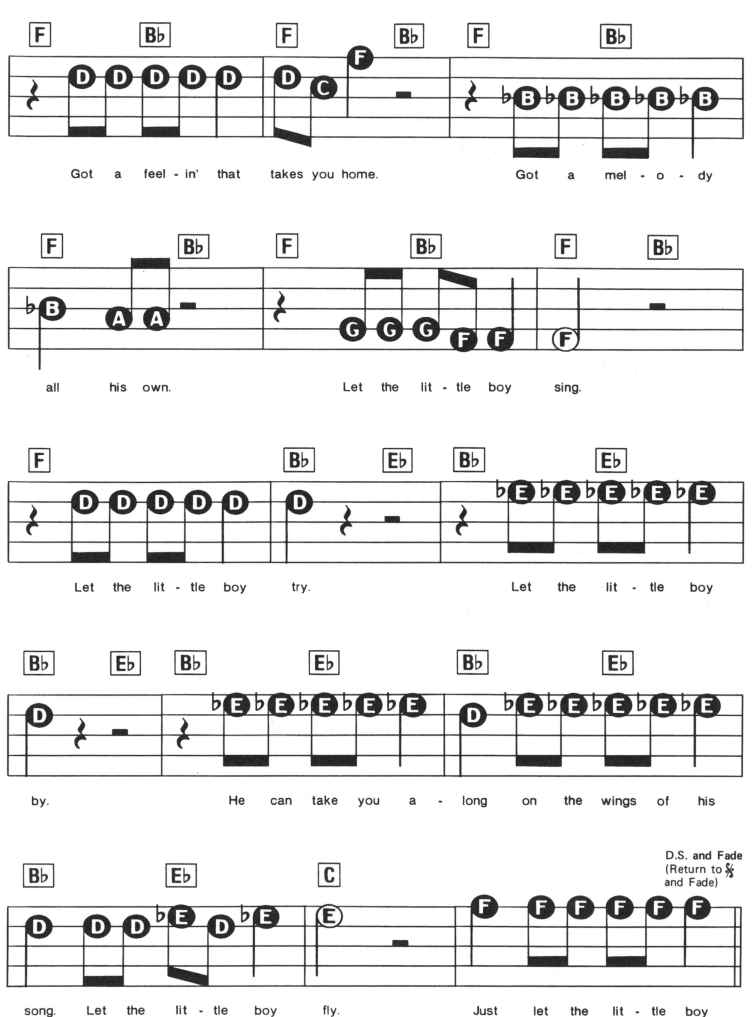

Longfellow Serenade

Registration 1
Rhythm: Ballad or Fox Trot

Words and Music by
Neil Diamond

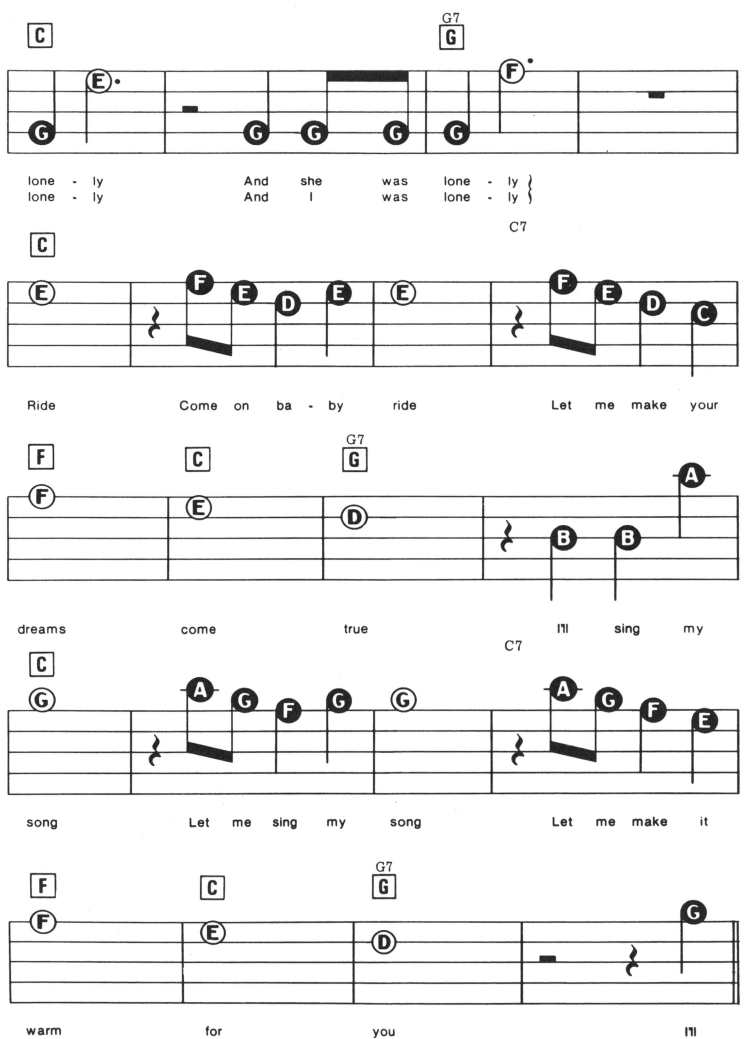

lone - ly   And   she   was   lone - ly
lone - ly   And   I   was   lone - ly

Ride   Come on ba - by ride   Let me make your

dreams   come   true   I'll sing my

song   Let me sing my song   Let me make it

warm   for   you   I'll

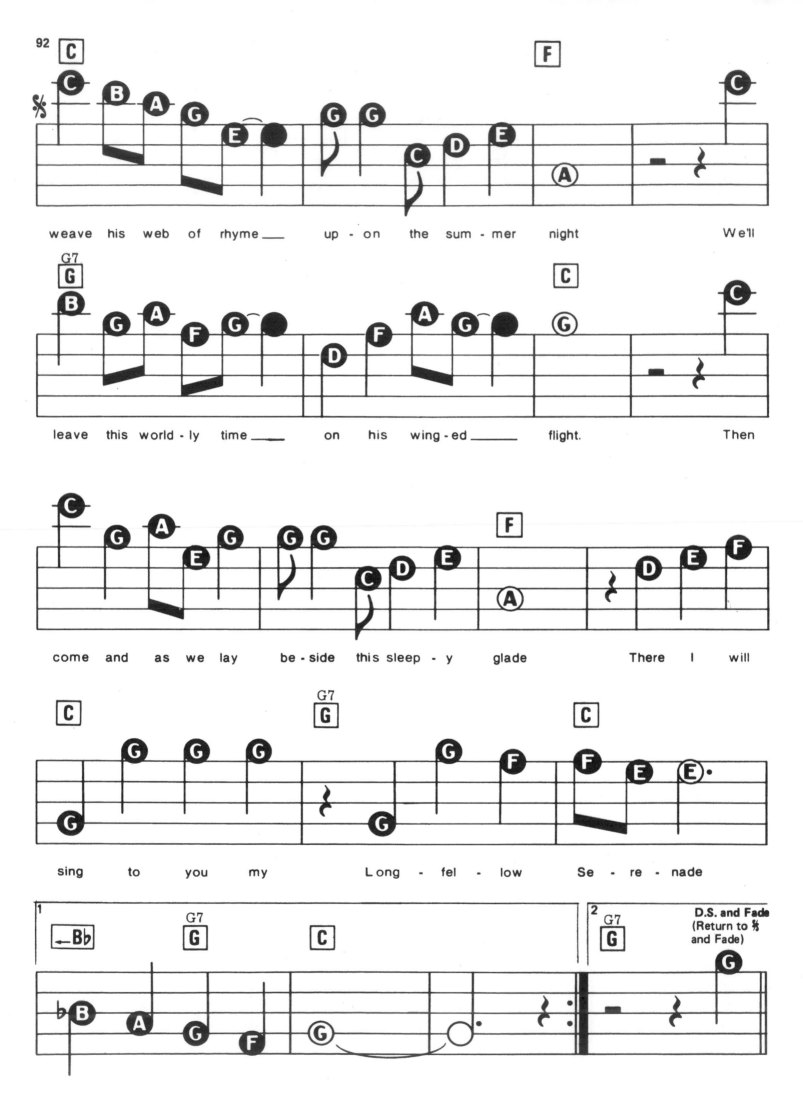

Love On The Rocks

From the Motion Picture "The Jazz Singer"

Registration 4
Rhythm: Rock

Words and Music by
Neil Diamond and Gilbert Becaud

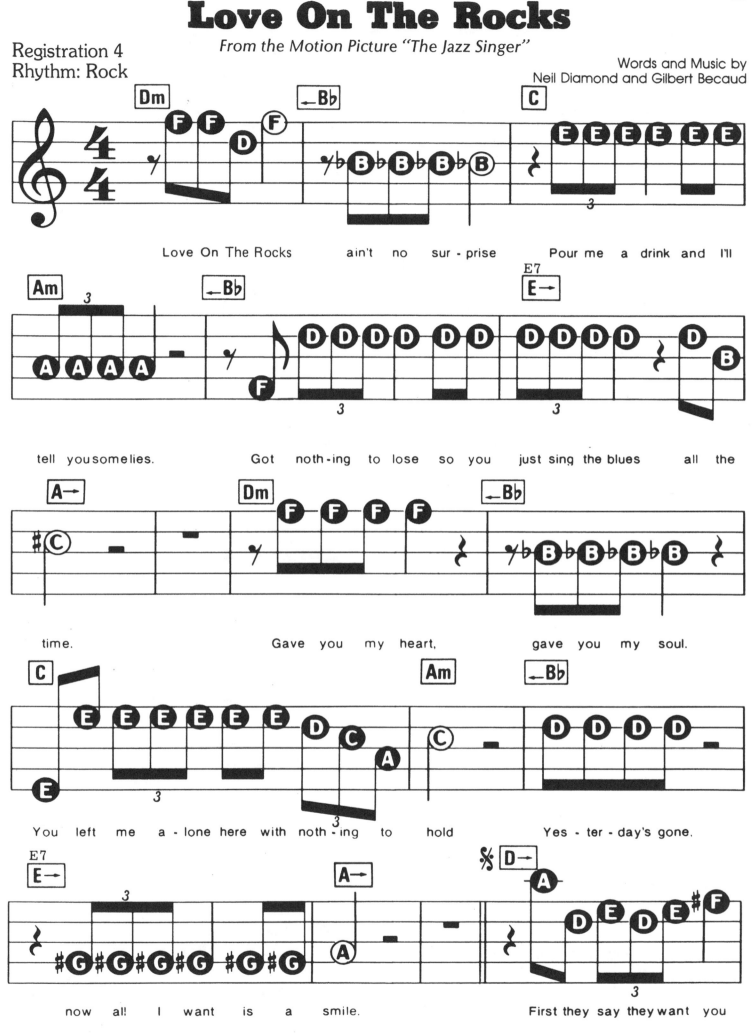

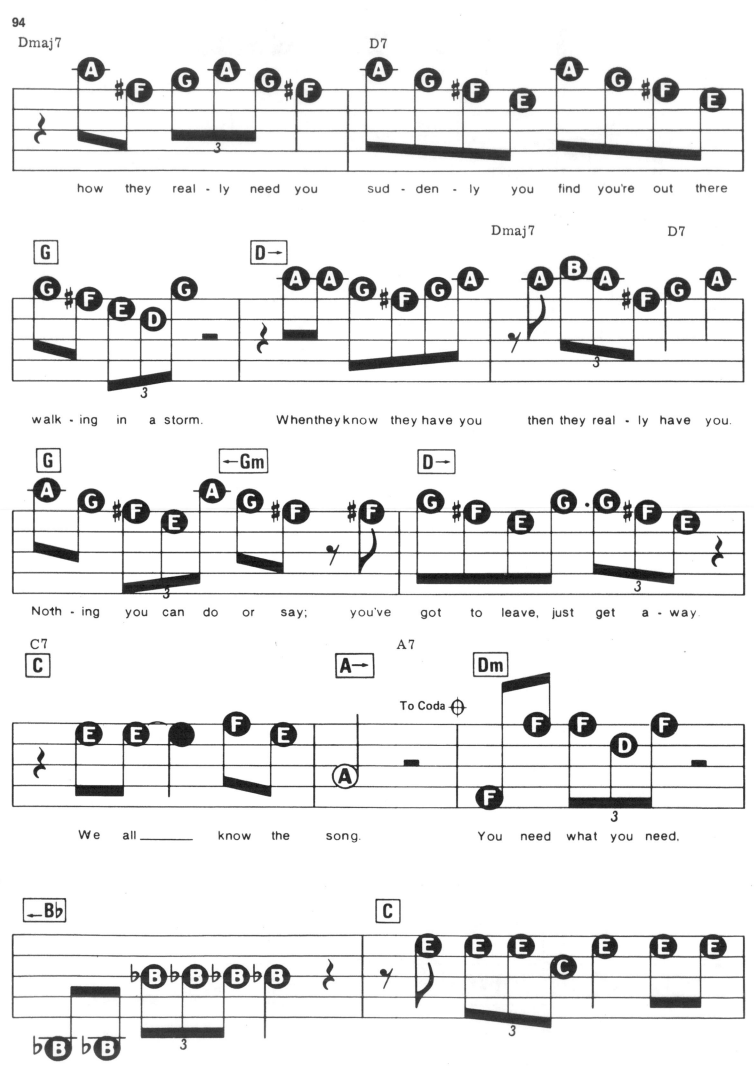

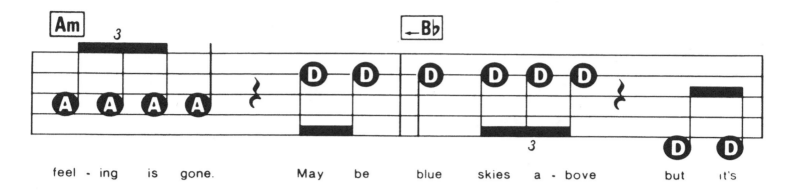

feel - ing is gone. May be blue skies a - bove but it's

D.S. al Coda (Return to 𝄋
Play to ⊕ and skip to Coda)

CODA ⊕

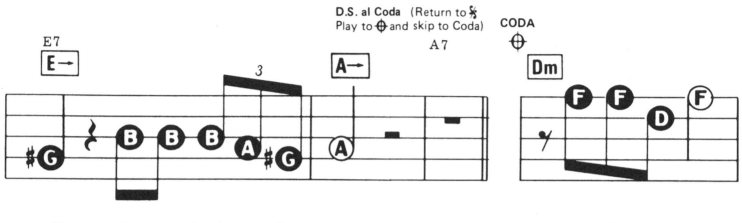

cold when your love's on the rocks.

Love On The Rocks

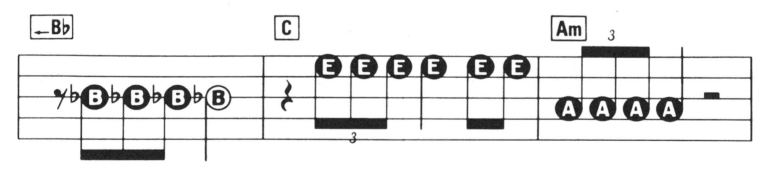

ain't no sur - prise Pour me a drink and I'll tell you some lies.

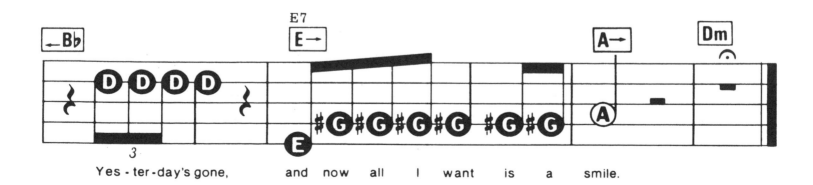

Yes - ter-day's gone, and now all I want is a smile.

On The Robert E. Lee

From the Motion Picture "The Jazz Singer"

Registration 1
Rhythm: Swing

Words and Music by
Neil Diamond and Gilbert Becaud

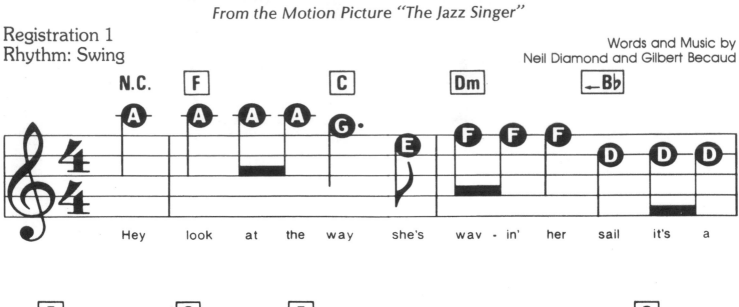

Hey look at the way she's wav - in' her sail it's a

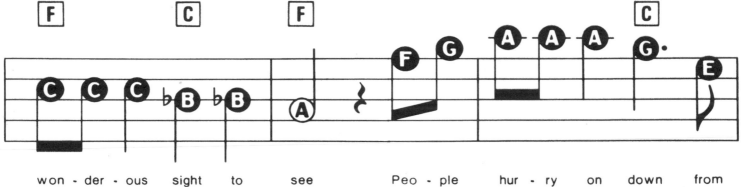

won - der - ous sight to see Peo - ple hur - ry on down from

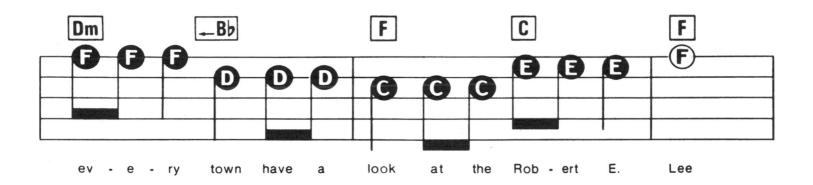

ev - e - ry town have a look at the Rob - ert E. Lee

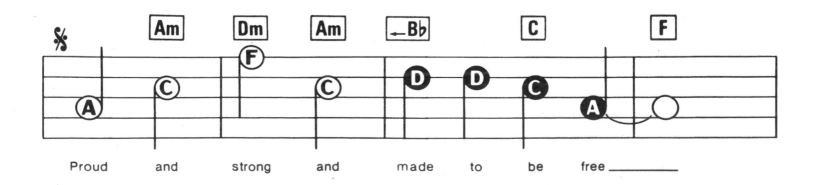

Proud and strong and made to be free _____

97

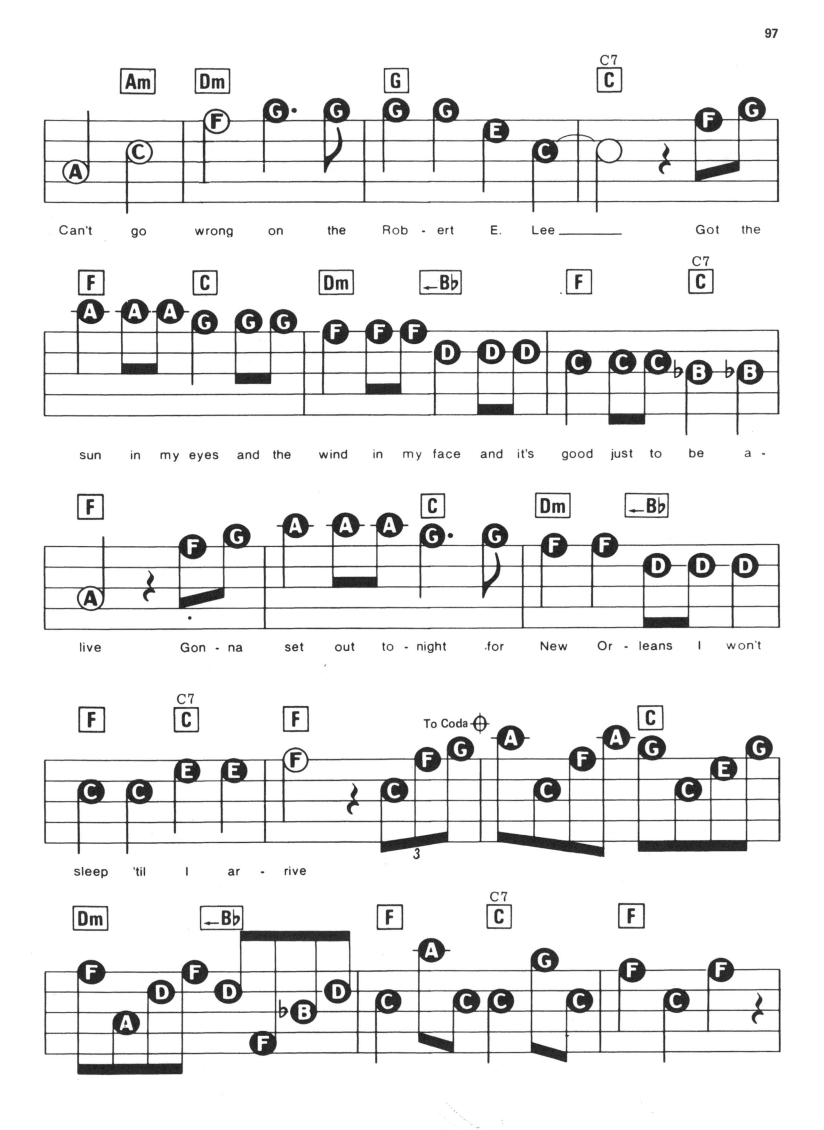

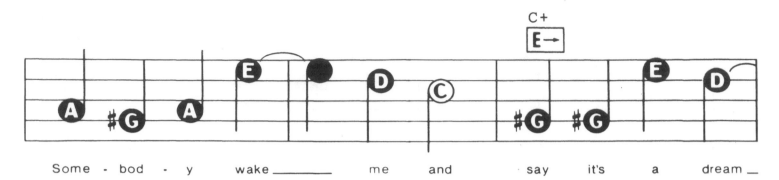

Some - bod - y wake _____ me and say it's a dream _

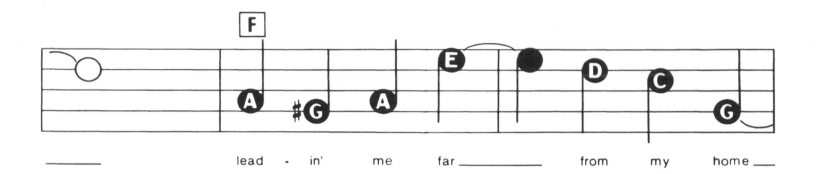

_____ lead - in' me far _____ from my home __

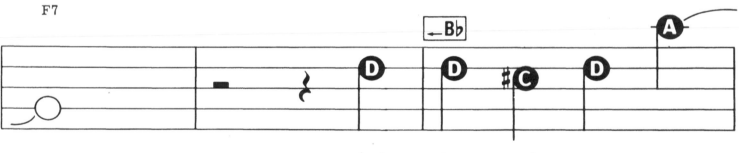

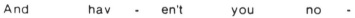

_____ And hav - en't you no -

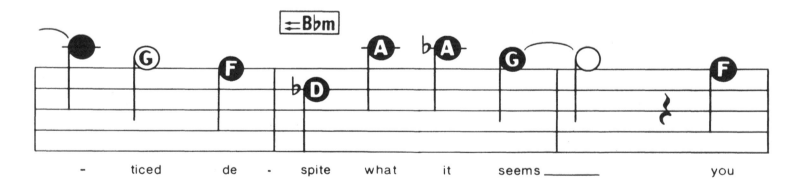

- ticed de - spite what it seems _____ you

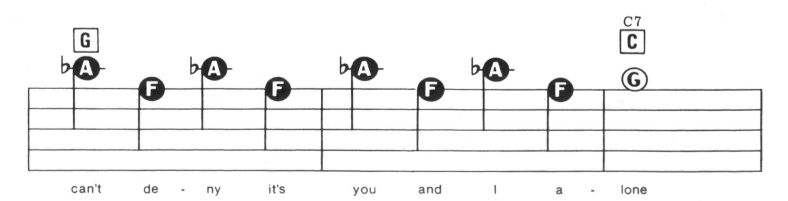

can't de - ny it's you and I a - lone

99

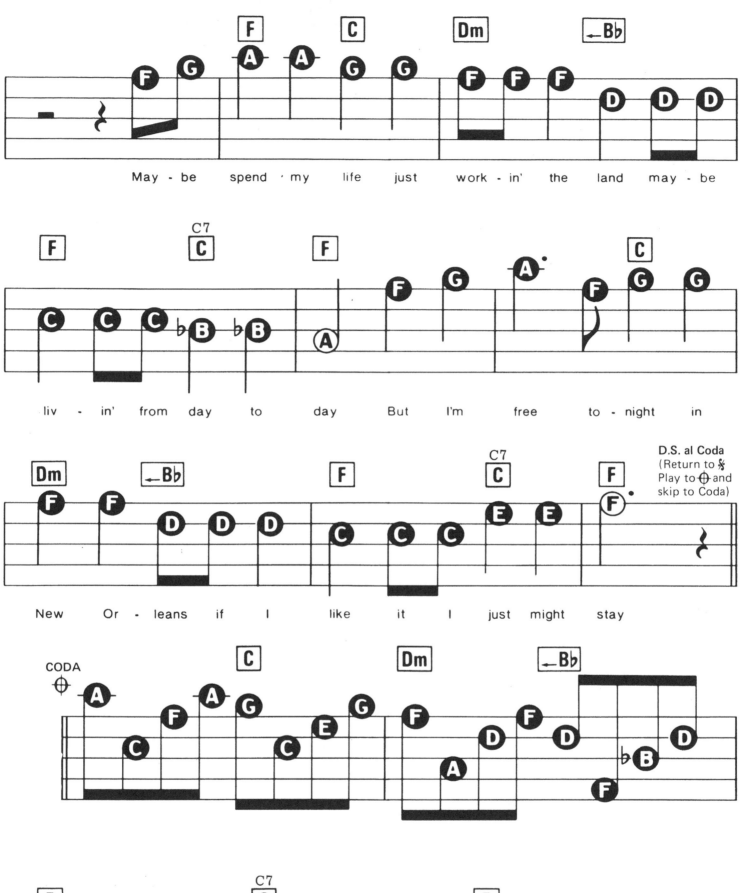

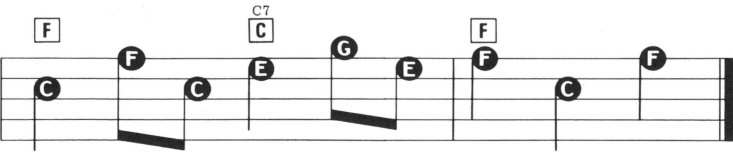

On The Way To The Sky

Registration 8
Rhythm: Waltz

Words and Music by Neil Diamond
and Carole Bayer Sager

N.C. | F | Gm

C A A A A C ♭B A G G G ♭B A G

I'm back on my feet a - gain Out on the street a - gain

F | Dm | Gm | C | F

F G A F C A G A ♭B G A A A

Look - ing for love on the way to the sky Some peo - ple

Gm | F | Dm

C ♭B A G G G ♭B A G F G A F D D

mov - ing up Some peo - ple stand - ing still Some hold their hand out and

Gm | C | B♭ | F

G A ♭B G A ♭B D E F C F D

some peo - ple nev - er will Lov - ers and li - ars con -

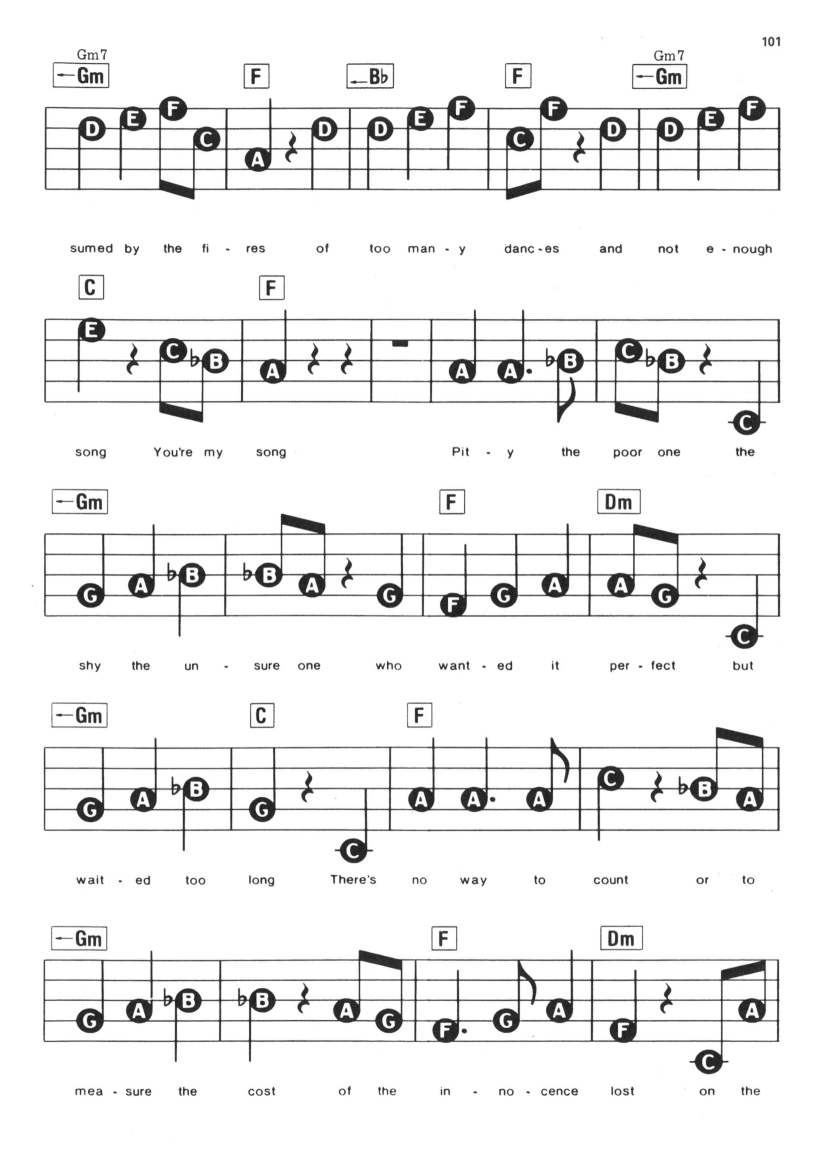

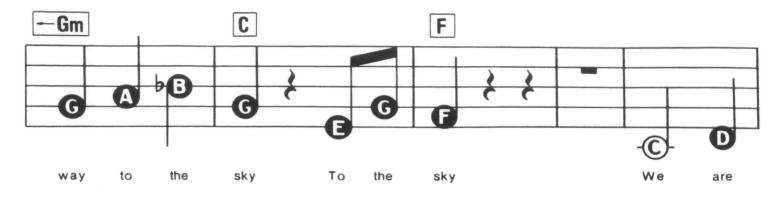

way   to   the   sky   To   the   sky   We   are

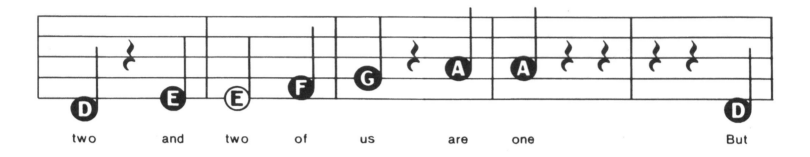

two   and   two   of   us   are   one   But

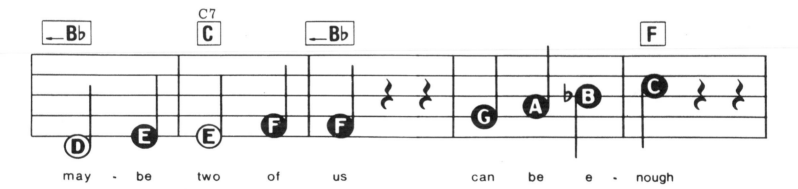

may - be   two   of   us   can   be   e - nough

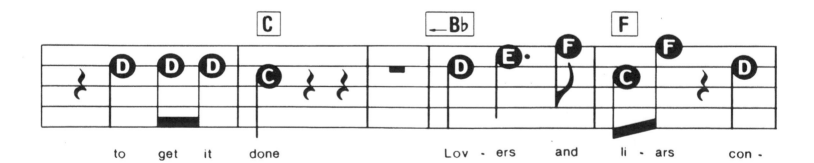

to   get   it   done   Lov - ers   and   li - ars   con -

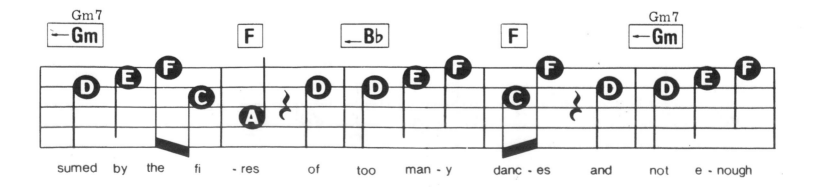

sumed   by   the   fi - res   of   too   man - y   danc - es   and   not   e - nough

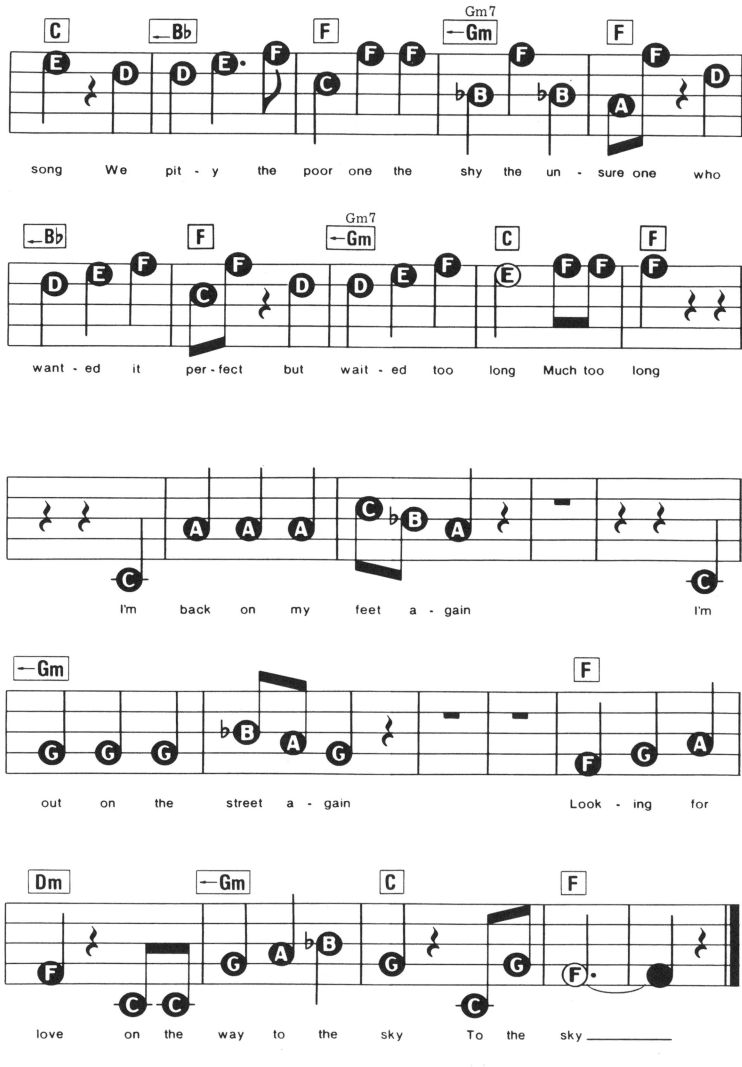

Play Me

Registration 2
Rhythm: Waltz

Words and Music by
Neil Diamond

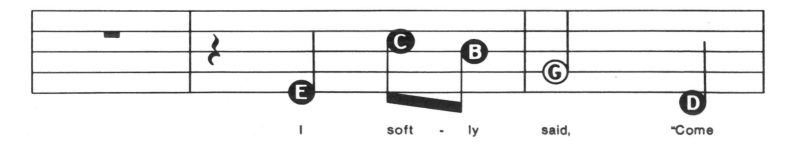

G

D D C B C D D

She was morn - ing and I was

C B C D D C B D

night time. I one day woke up to

G **C**

D D C B C B G

find her ly - in' be - side my bed.

C B E G D

I soft - ly said, "Come

106

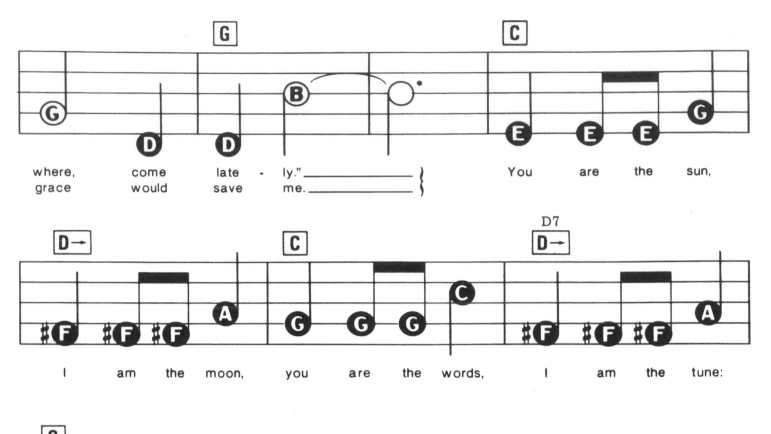

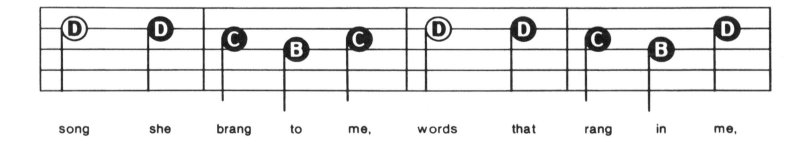

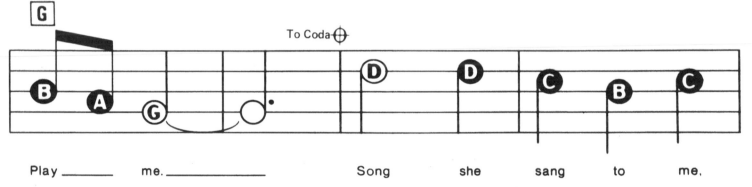

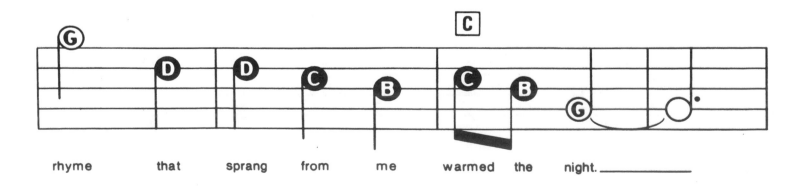

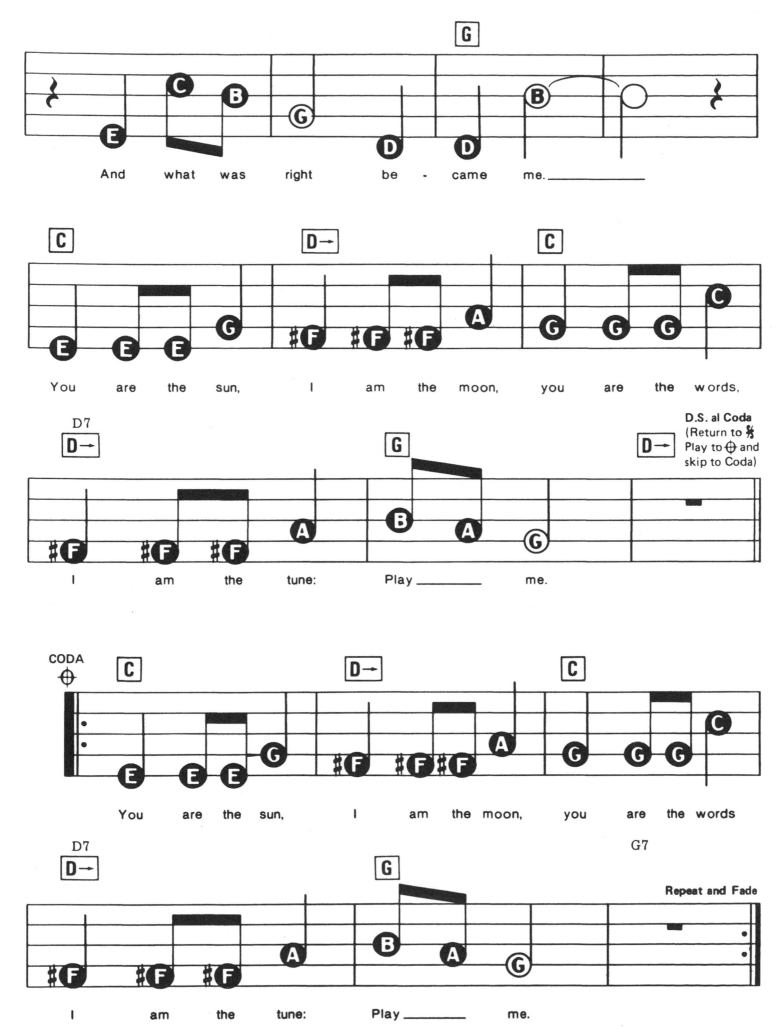

Porcupine Pie

Registration 5
Rhythm: Fox Trot or Rock

Words and Music by
Neil Diamond

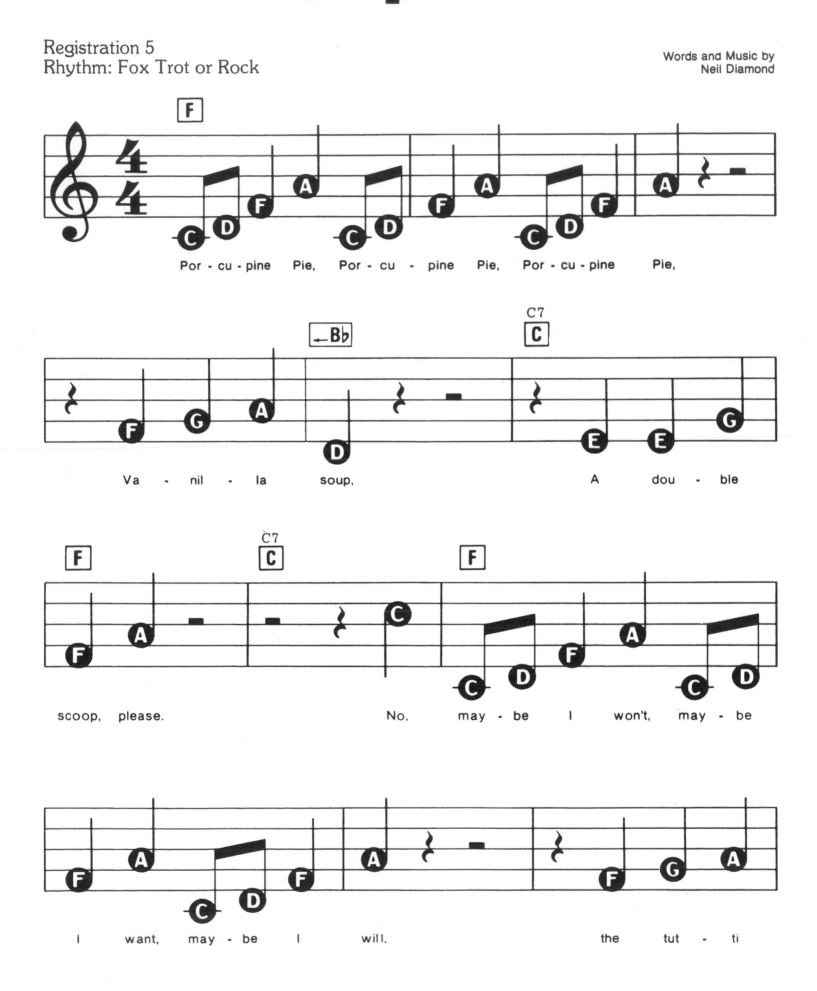

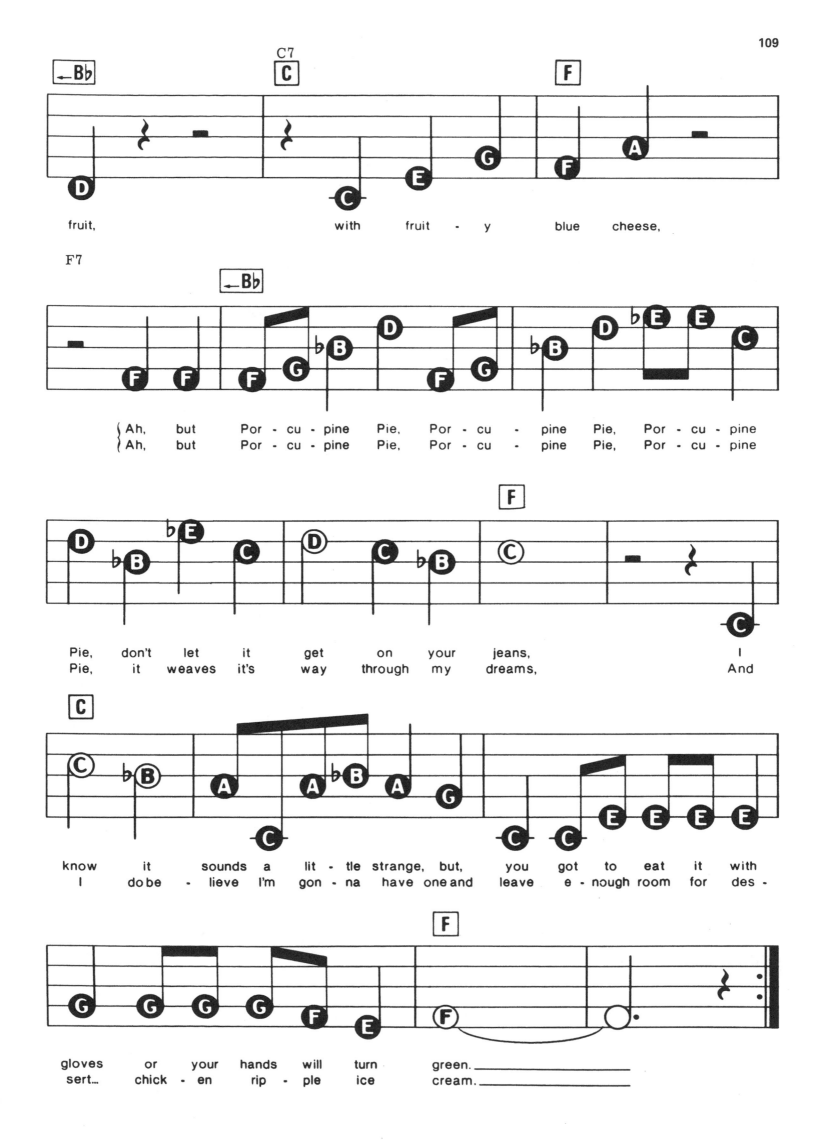

Red, Red Wine

Registration 2
Rhythm: Country

Words and Music by
Neil Diamond

111

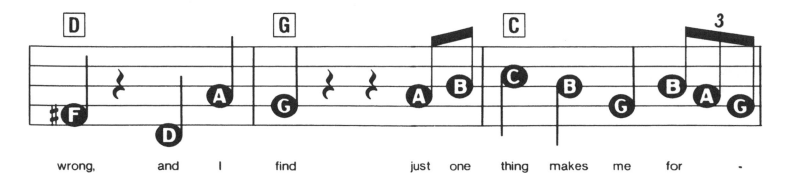

wrong, and I find just one thing makes me for -

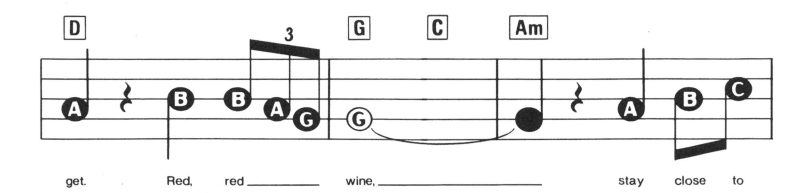

get. Red, red _____ wine, _____ stay close to

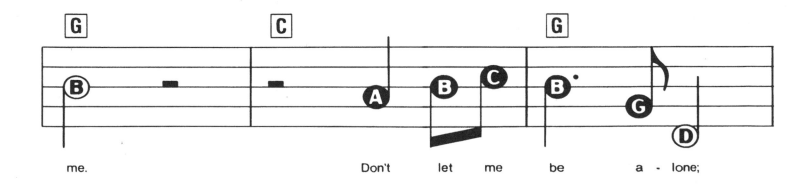

me. Don't let me be a - lone;

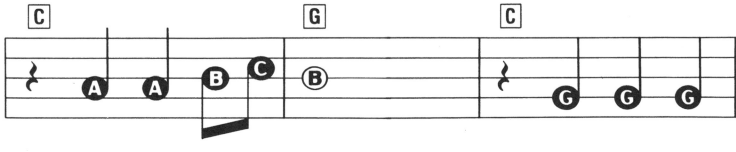

it's tear - ing a - part my blue, blue

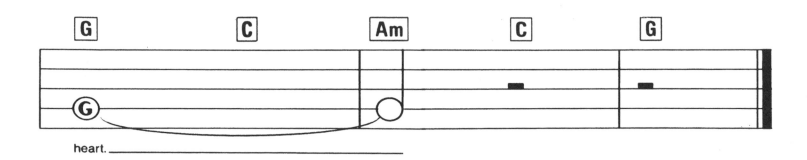

heart. _____

Rosemary's Wine

Registration 2
Rhythm: Ballad or Fox Trot

Words and Music by
Neil Diamond

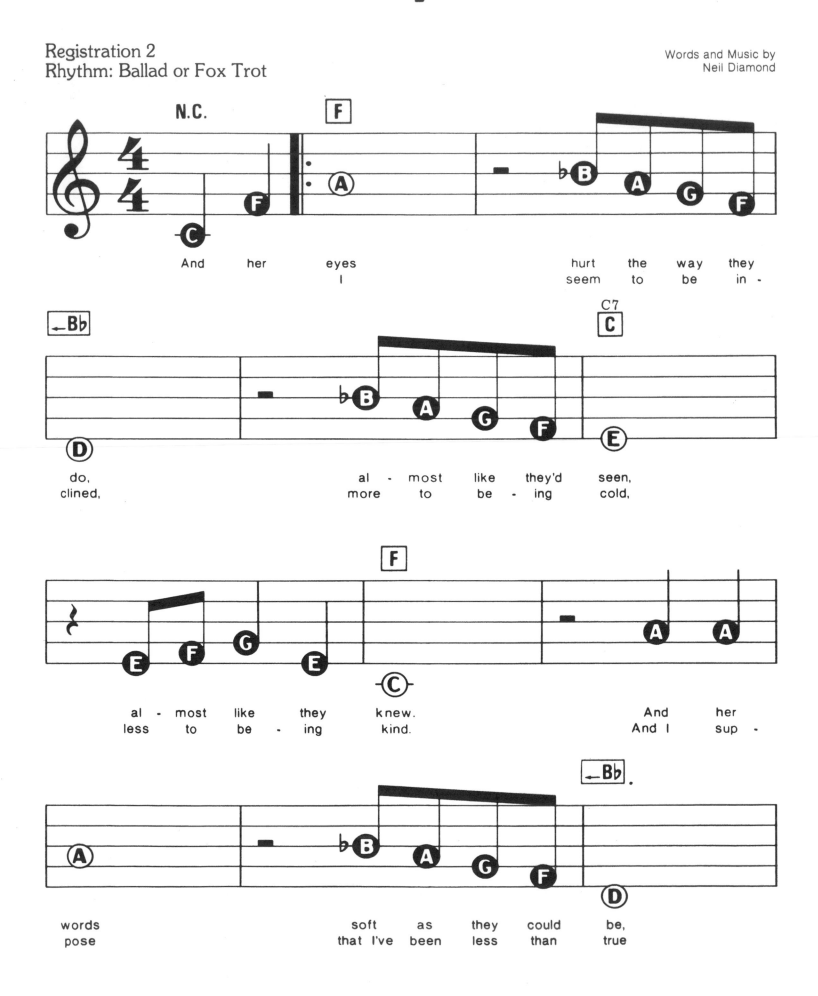

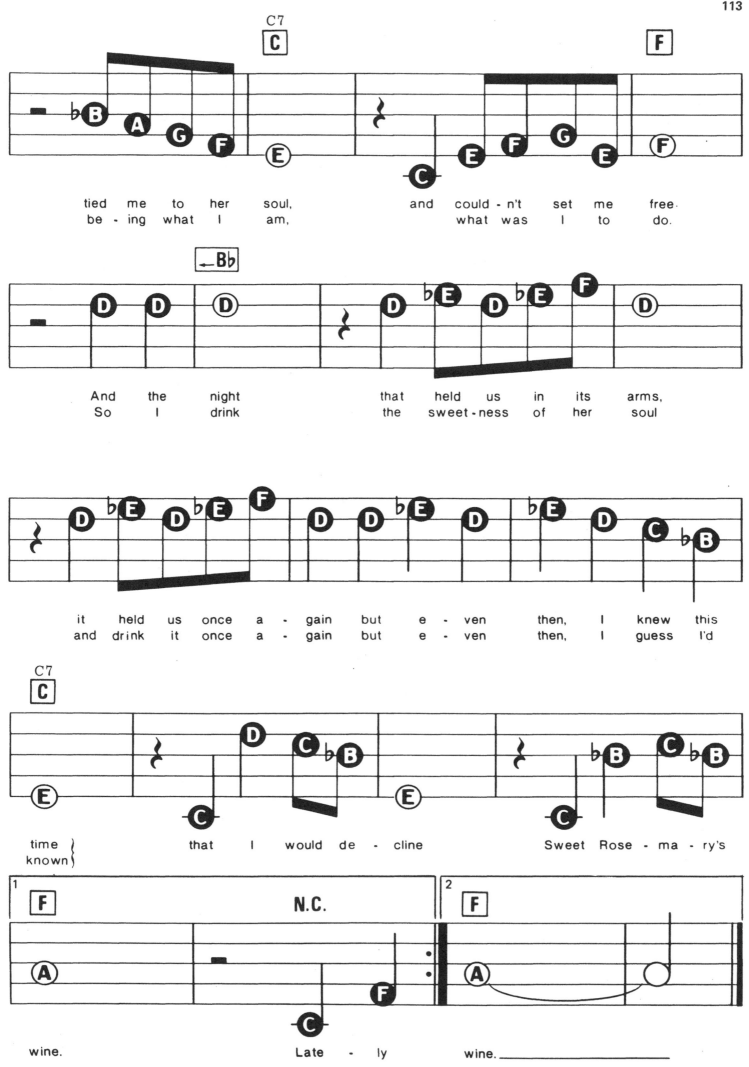

tied me to her soul, and could-n't set me free.
be - ing what I am, what was I to do.

And the night that held us in its arms,
So I drink the sweet-ness of her soul

it held us once a - gain but e - ven then, I knew this
and drink it once a - gain but e - ven then, I guess I'd

time }
known }
that I would de - cline Sweet Rose - ma - ry's

wine. Late - ly wine._____

September Morn

Registration 2
Rhythm: Ballad or Fox Trot

Words and Music by
Neil Diamond and Gilbert Becaud

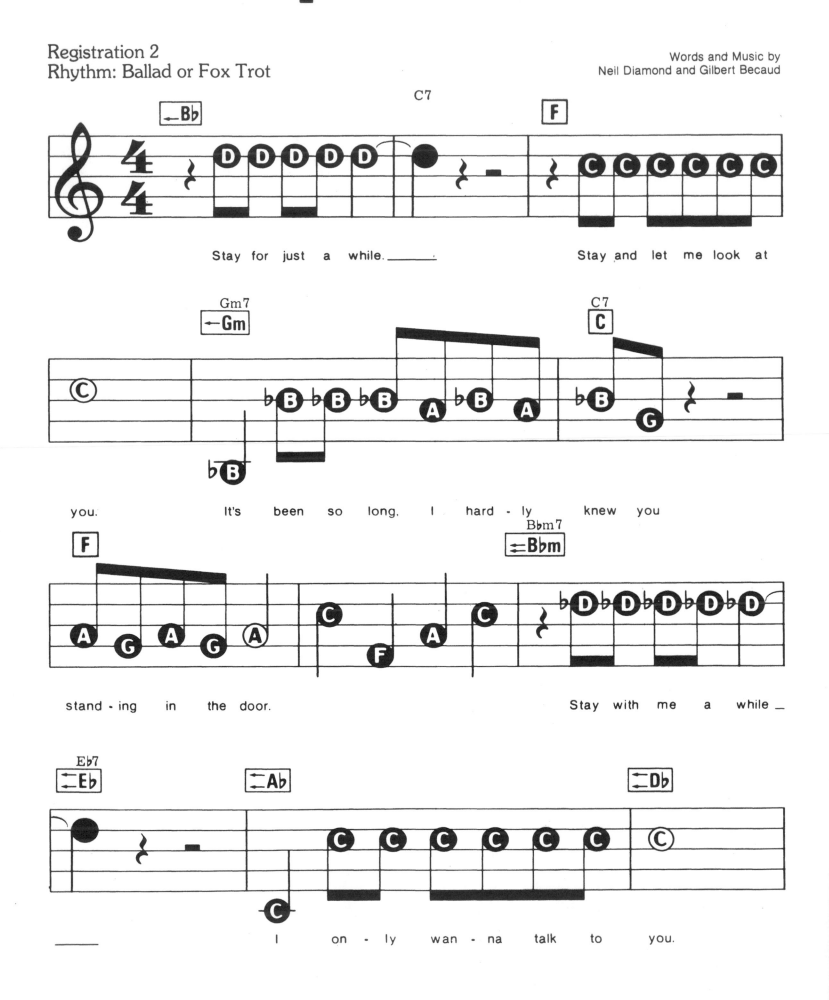

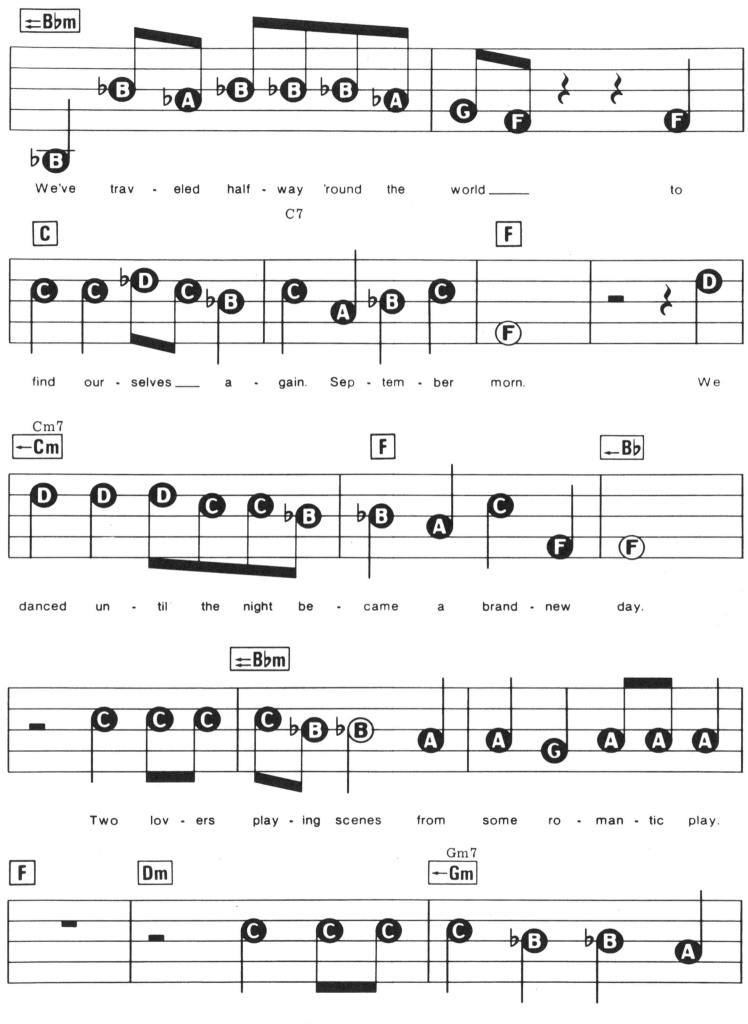

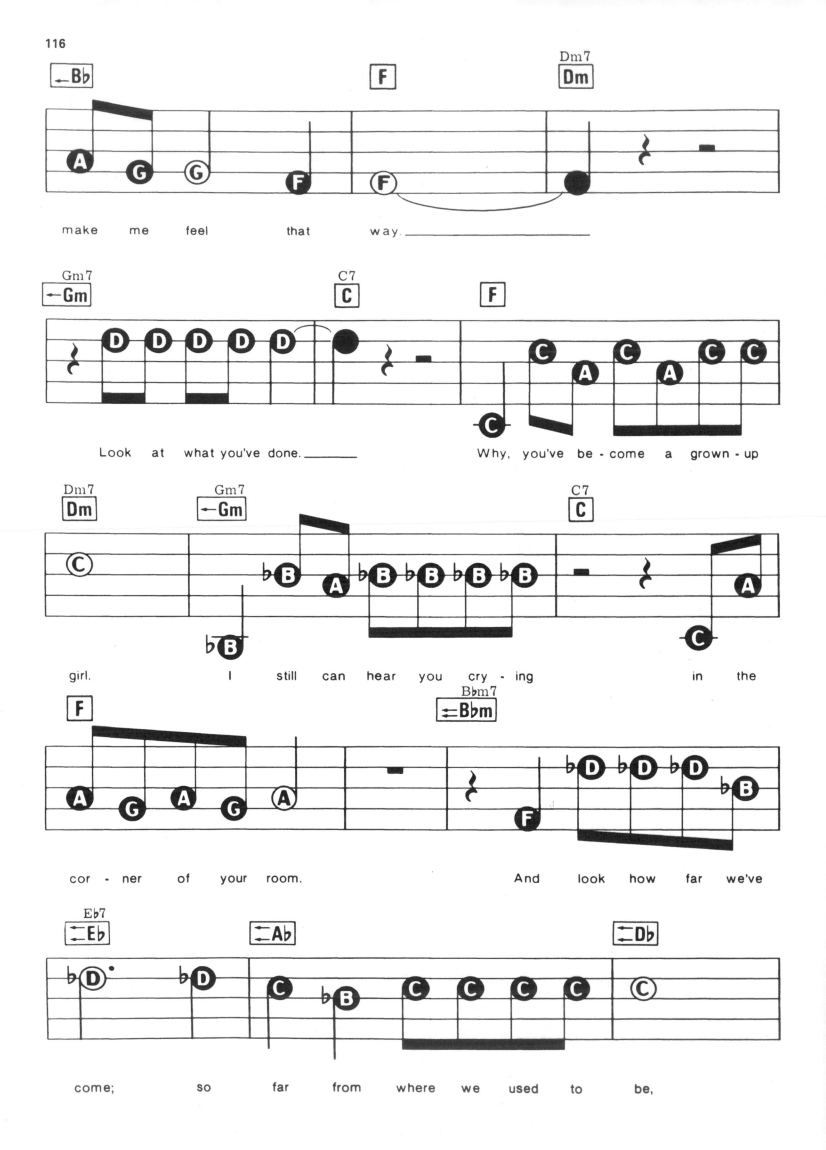

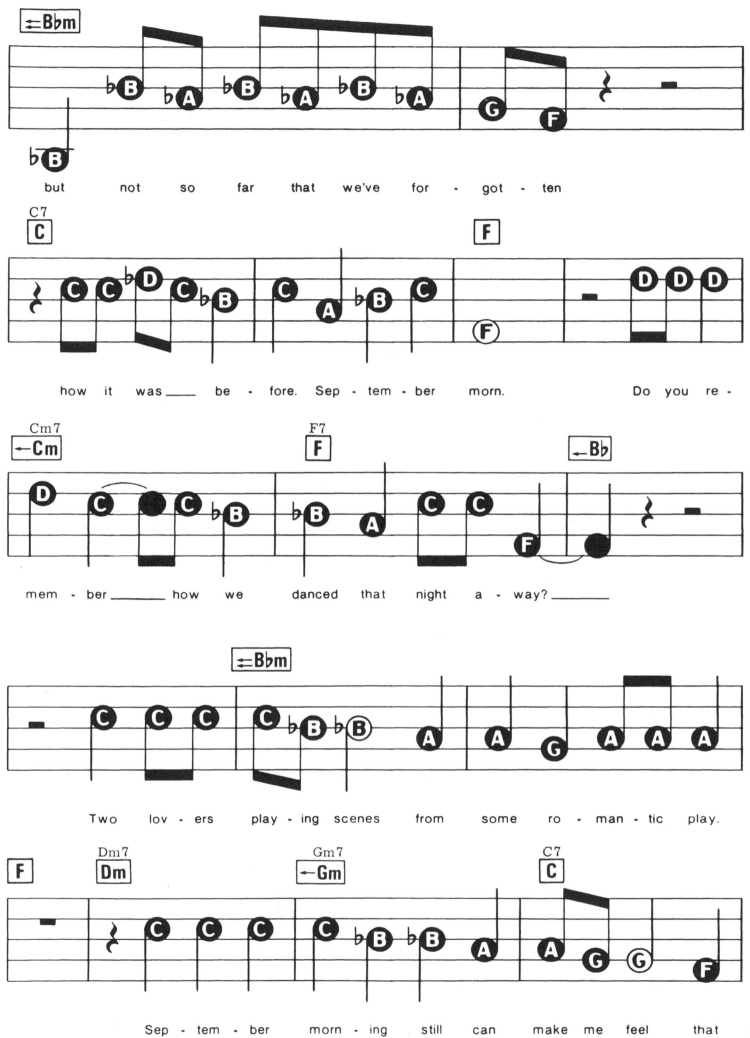

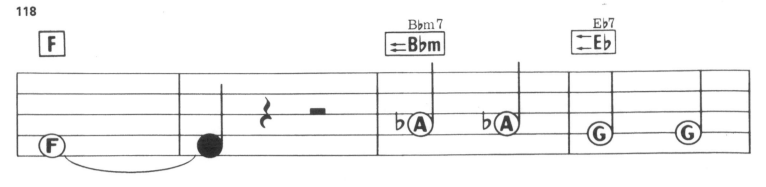

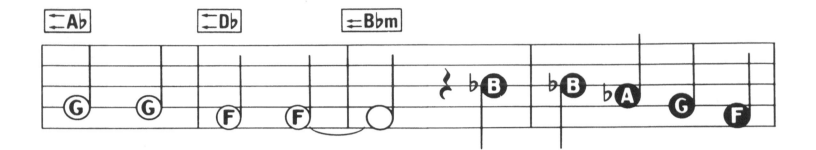

way. _____

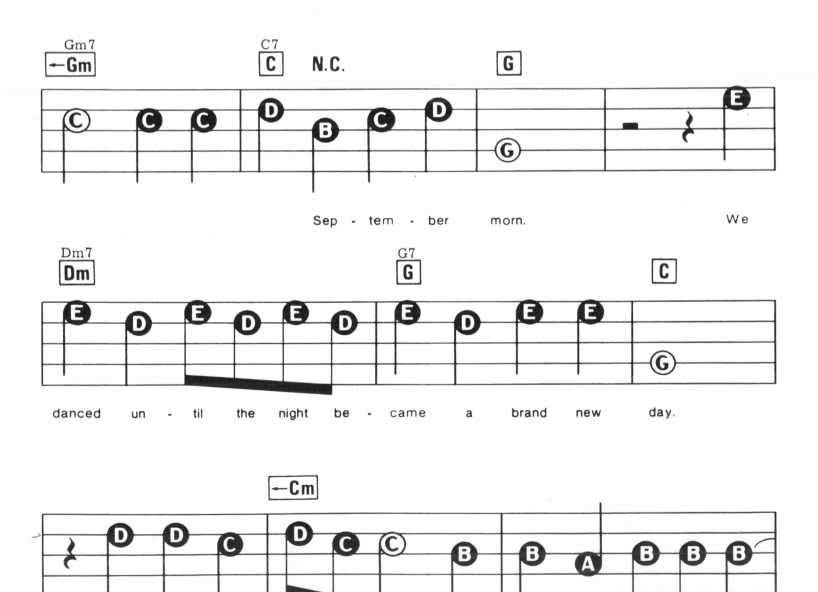

Sep - tem - ber morn. We

danced un - til the night be - came a brand new day.

Two lov - ers play - ing scenes from some ro - man - tic play. __

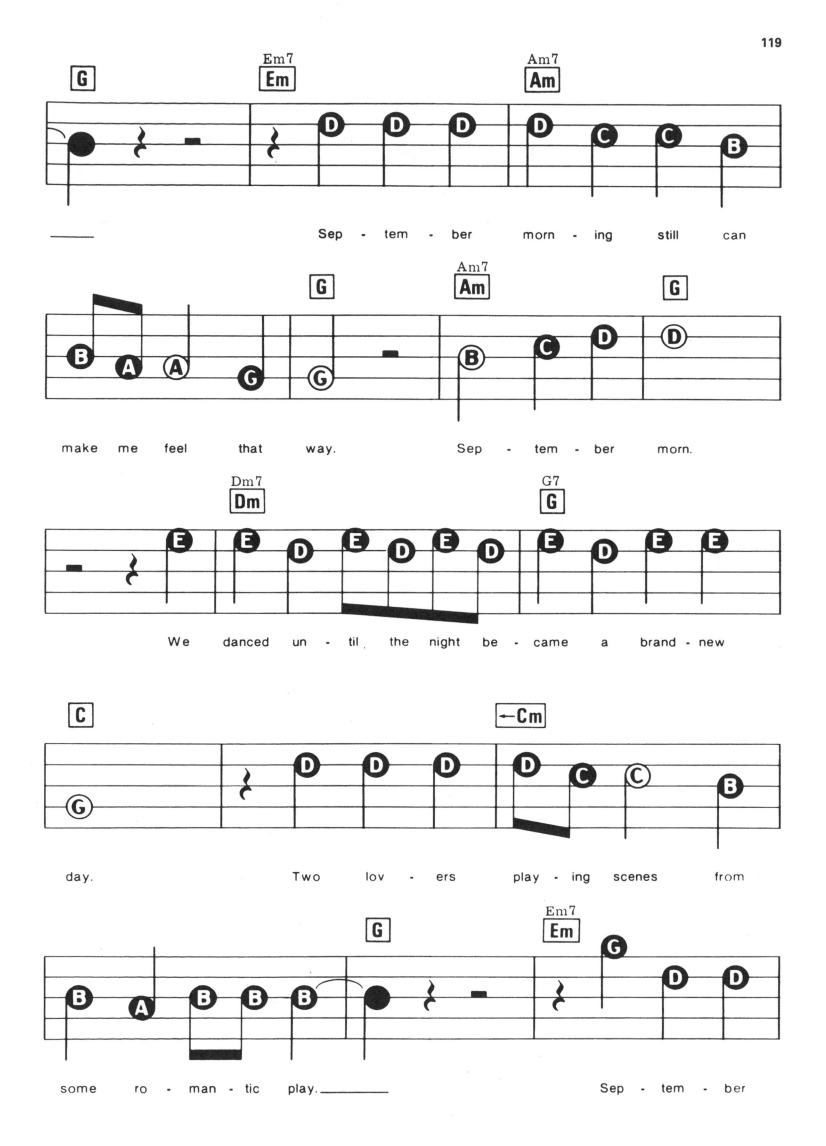

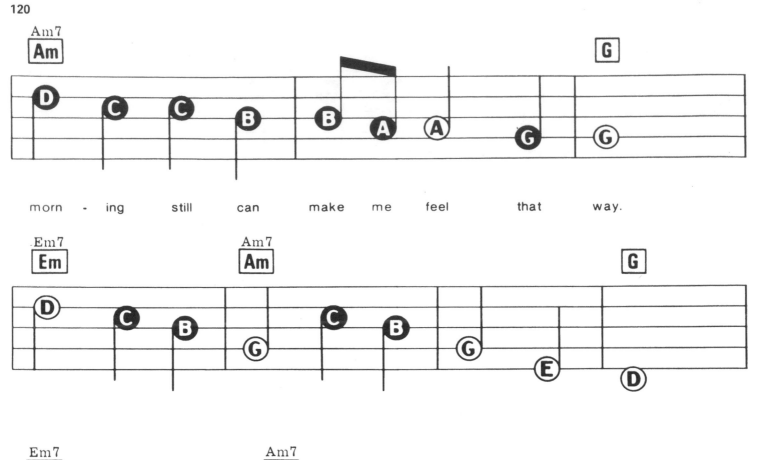

morn - ing   still   can   make   me   feel   that   way.

Sep - tem - ber   morn - ing   still   can   make   me   feel   that

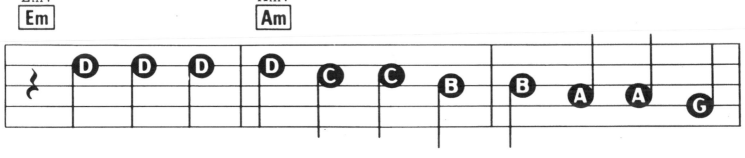

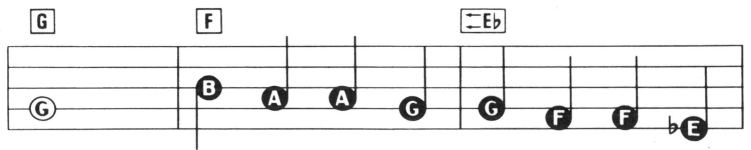

way.

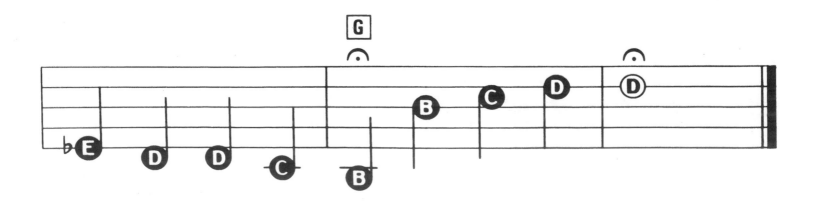

Stones

Registration 3
Rhythm: Rock or Latin

Words and Music by
Neil Diamond

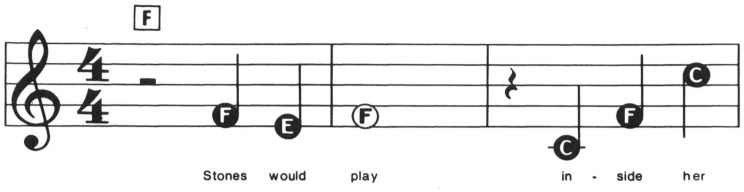

Stones would play   in - side her

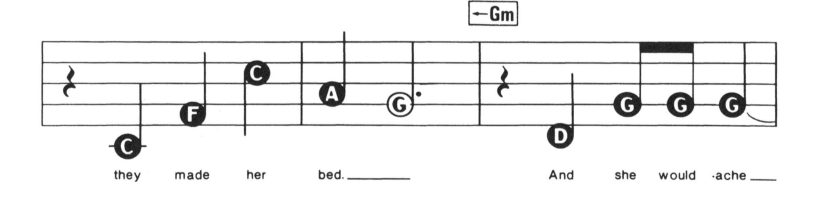

head,   and where she slept

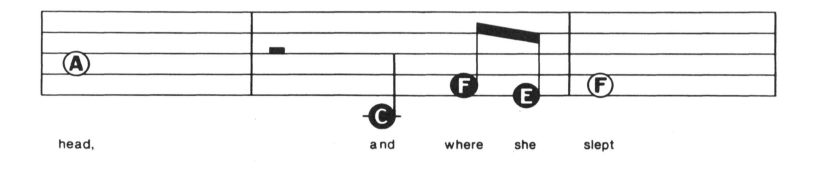

they made her bed._____   And she would ache ___

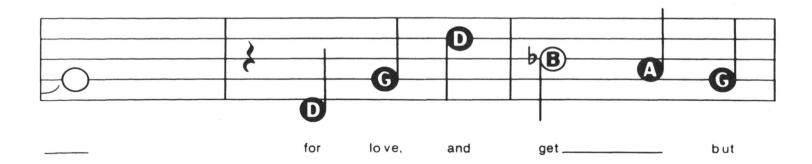

_____ for love, and get_____ but

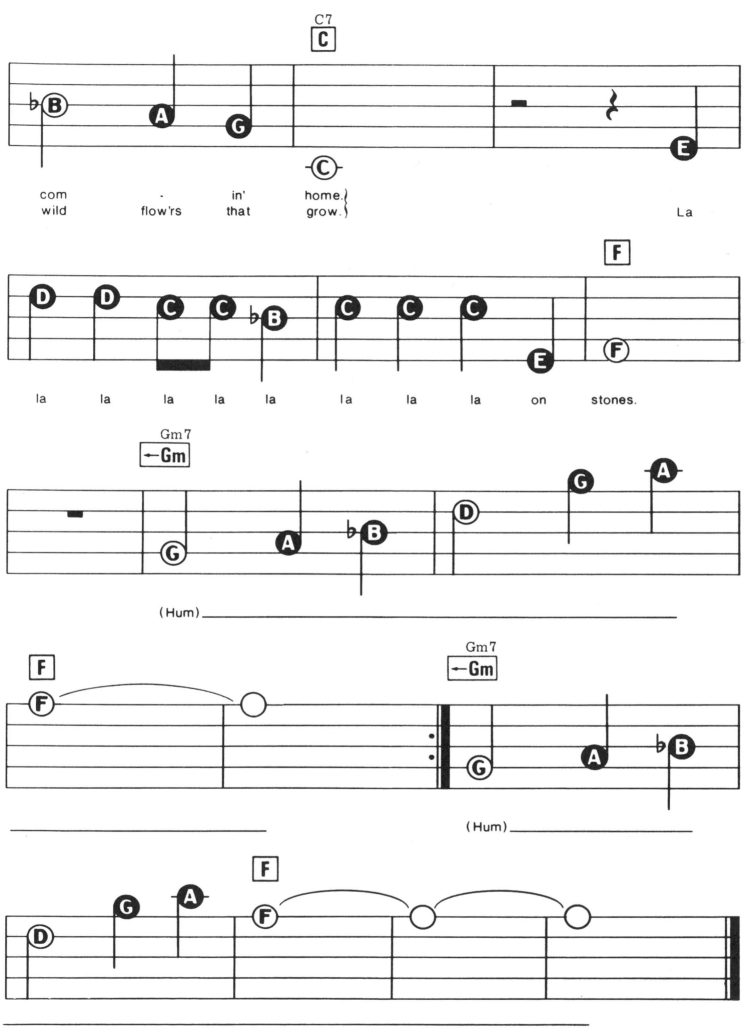

Shilo

Registration 5
Rhythm: Ballad or Country Western

Words and Music by
Neil Diamond

Skybird

Registration 10
Rhythm: Rock or Ballad

Words and Music by
Neil Diamond

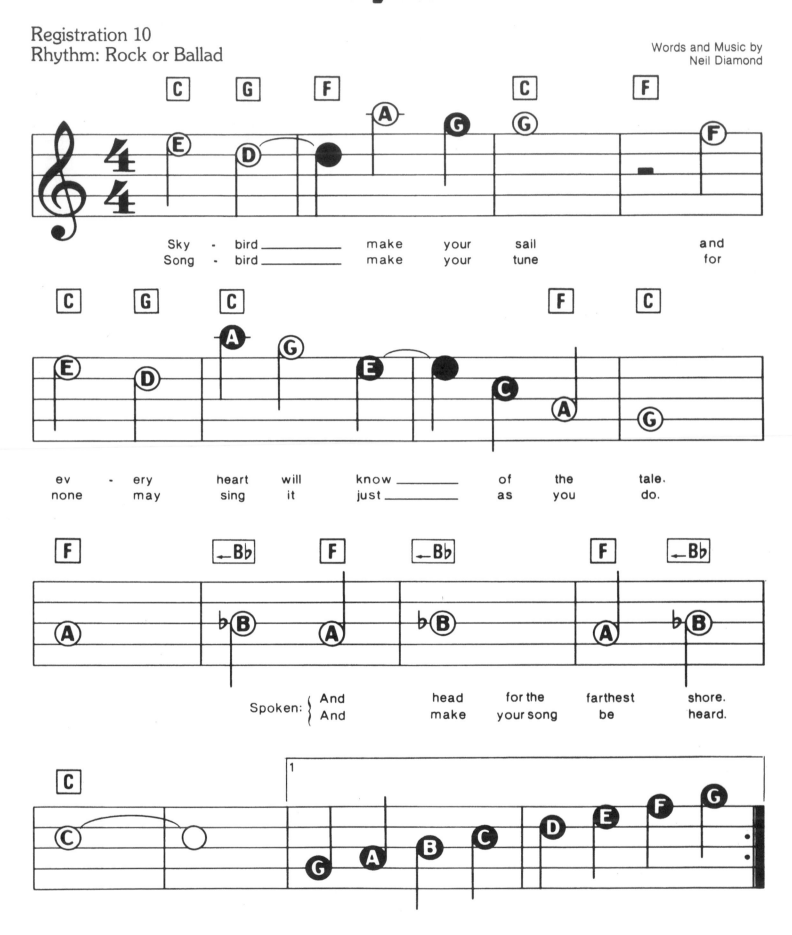

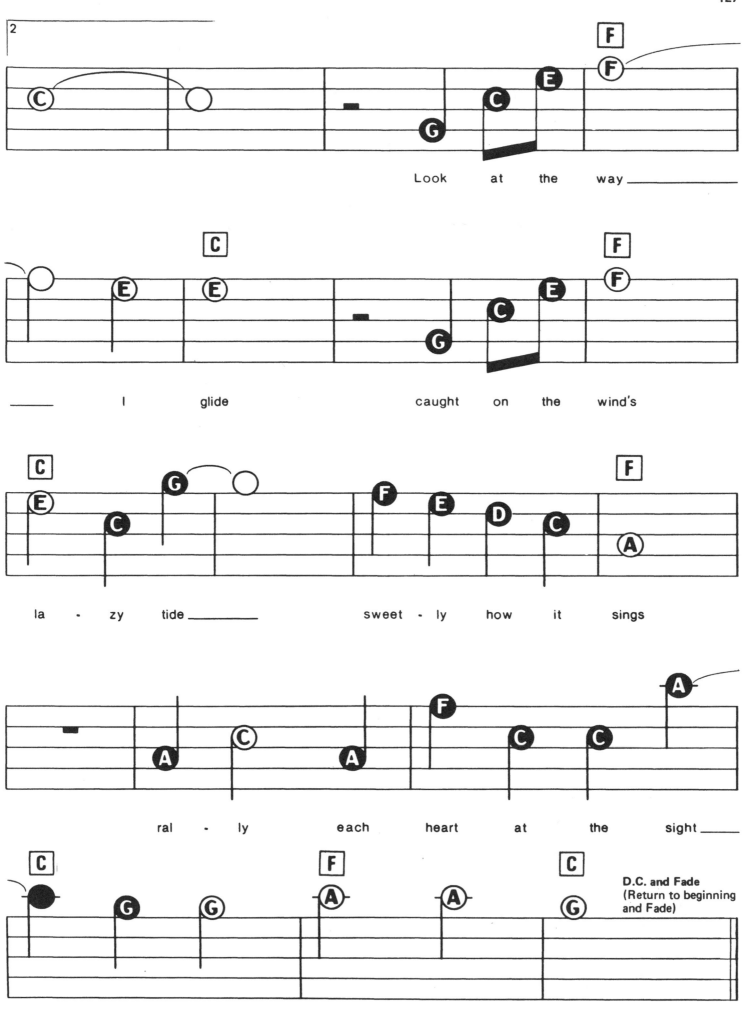

Look at the way _____

_____ I glide caught on the wind's

la - zy tide _____ sweet - ly how it sings

ral - ly each heart at the sight _____

_____ of your sil - ver wings.

D.C. and Fade
(Return to beginning
and Fade)

Solitary Man

Registration 10
Rhythm: Ballad or Fox Trot

Words and Music by
Neil Diamond

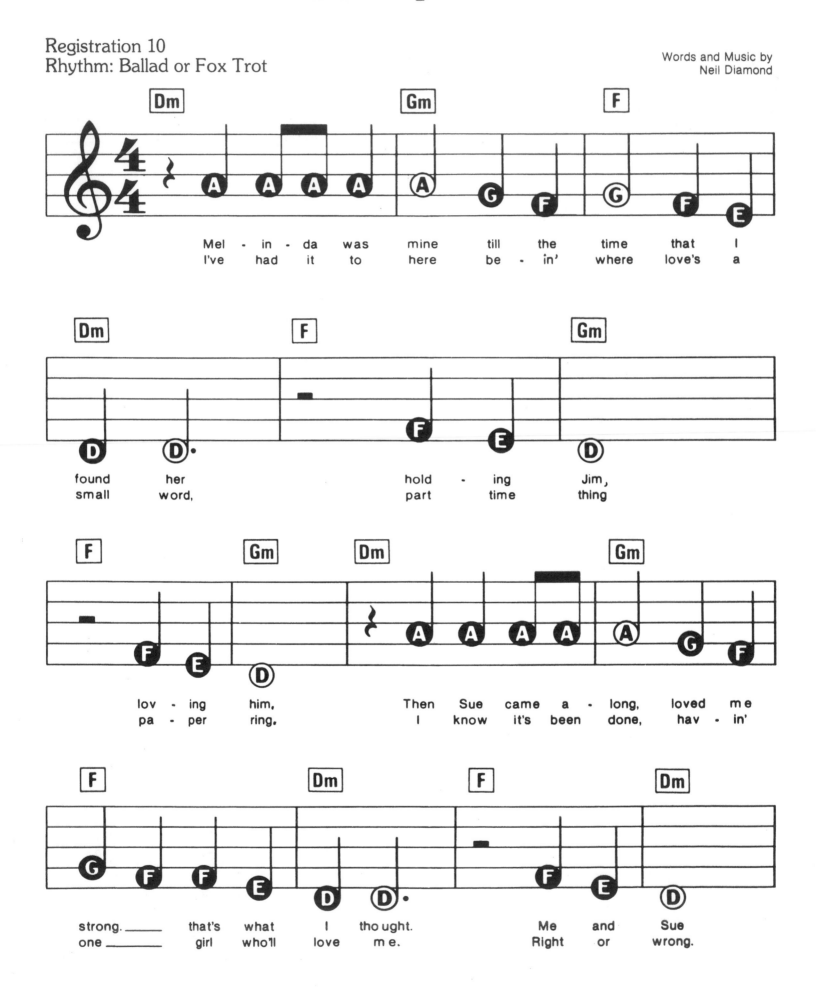

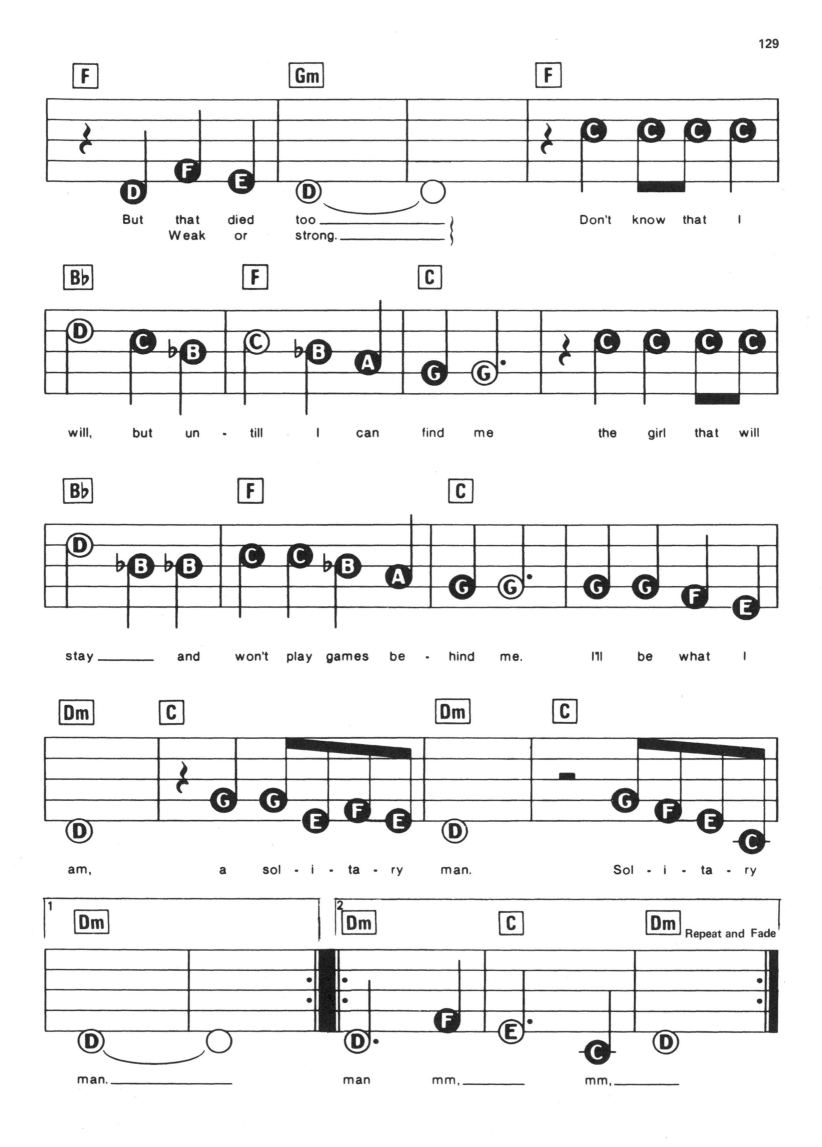

Song Sung Blue

Registration 2
Rhythm: Ballad or Fox Trot

Words and Music by
Neil Diamond

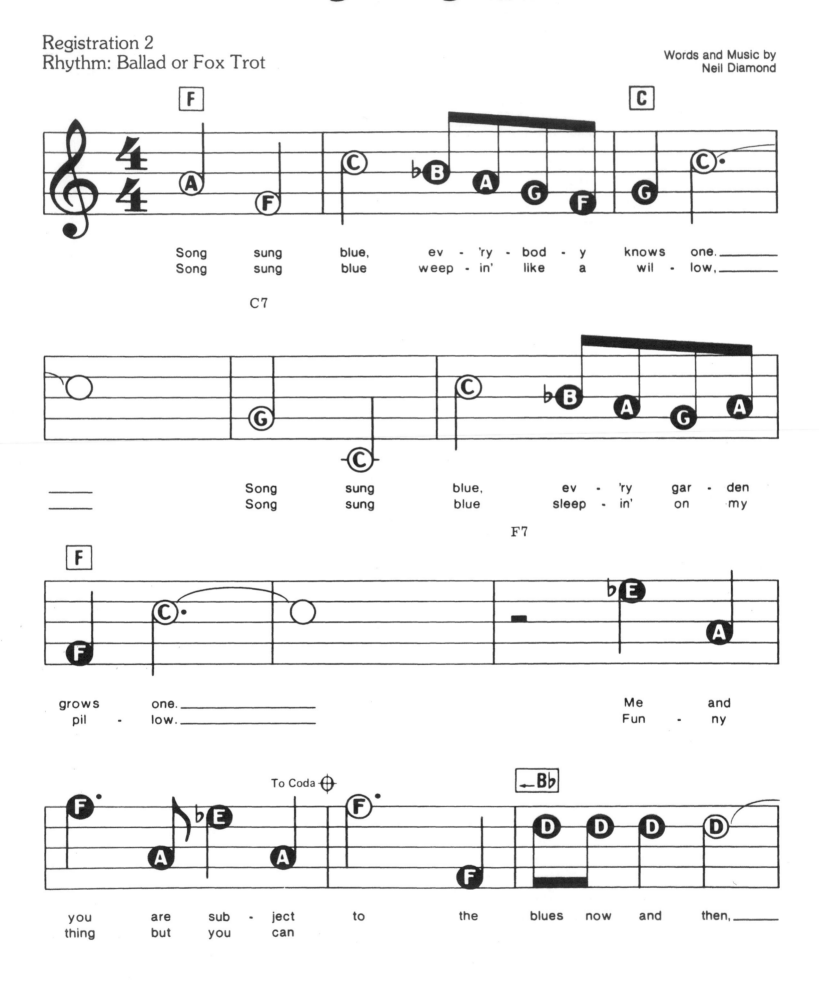

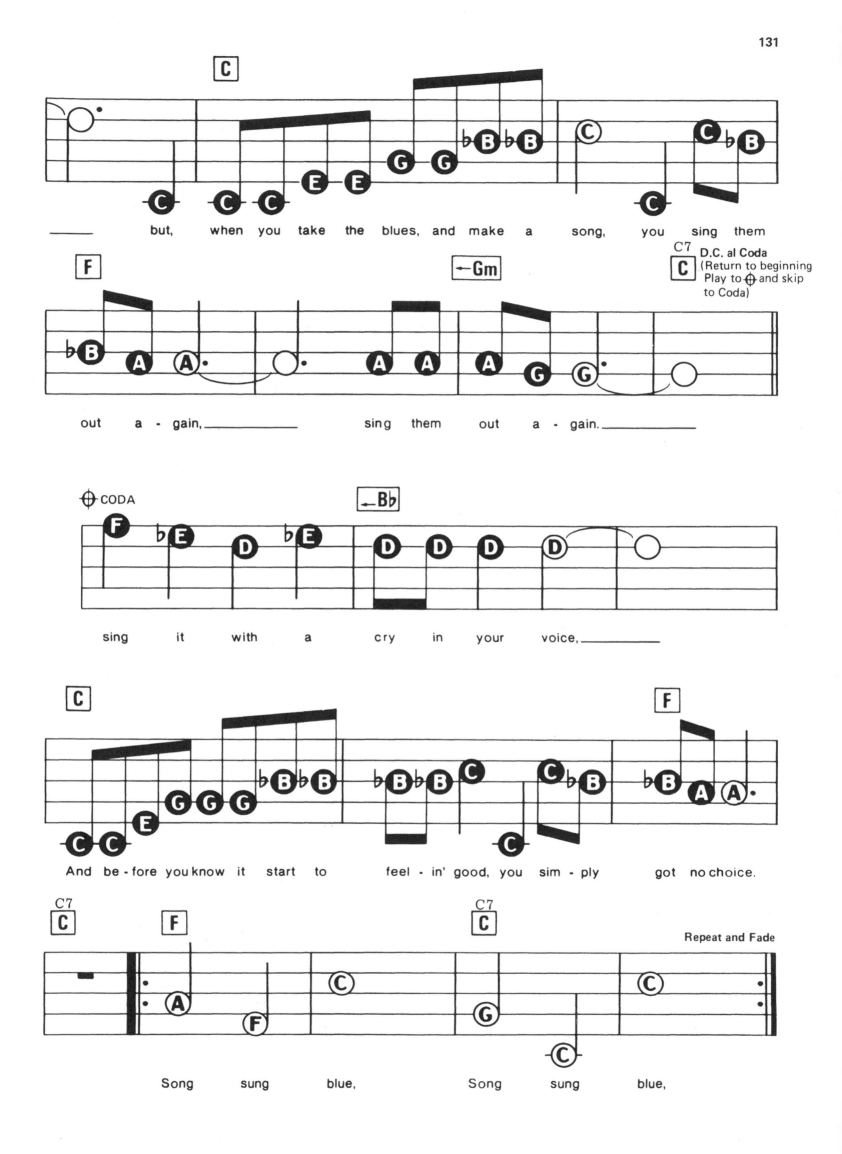

Sweet Caroline

Registration 4
Rhythm: Swing or Fox Trot

Words and Music by
Neil Diamond

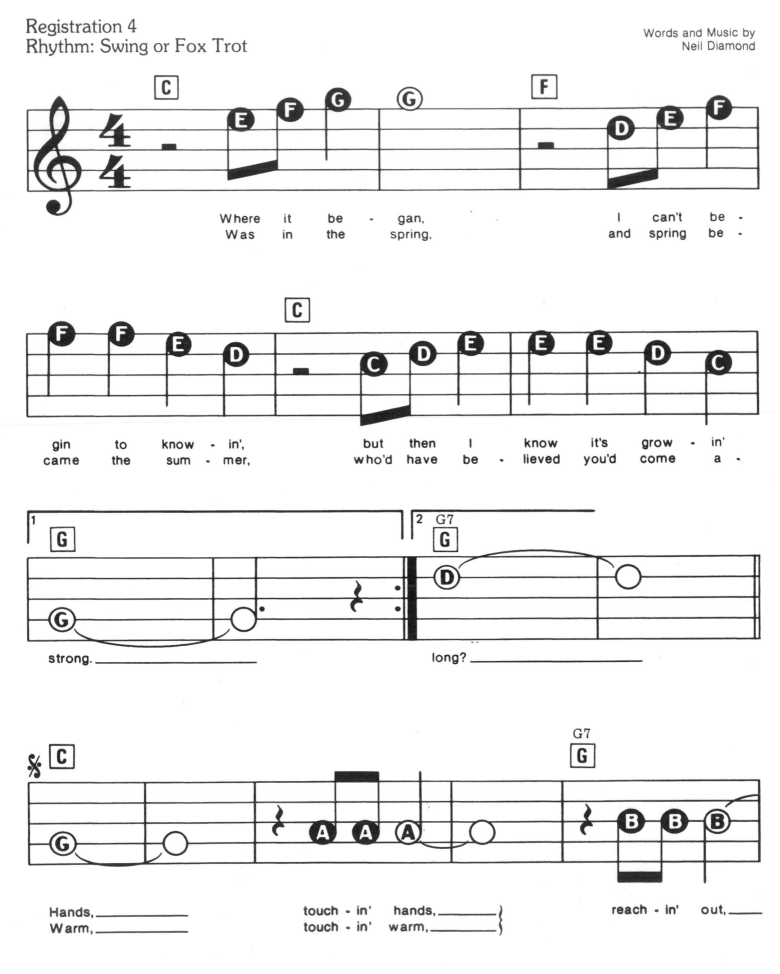

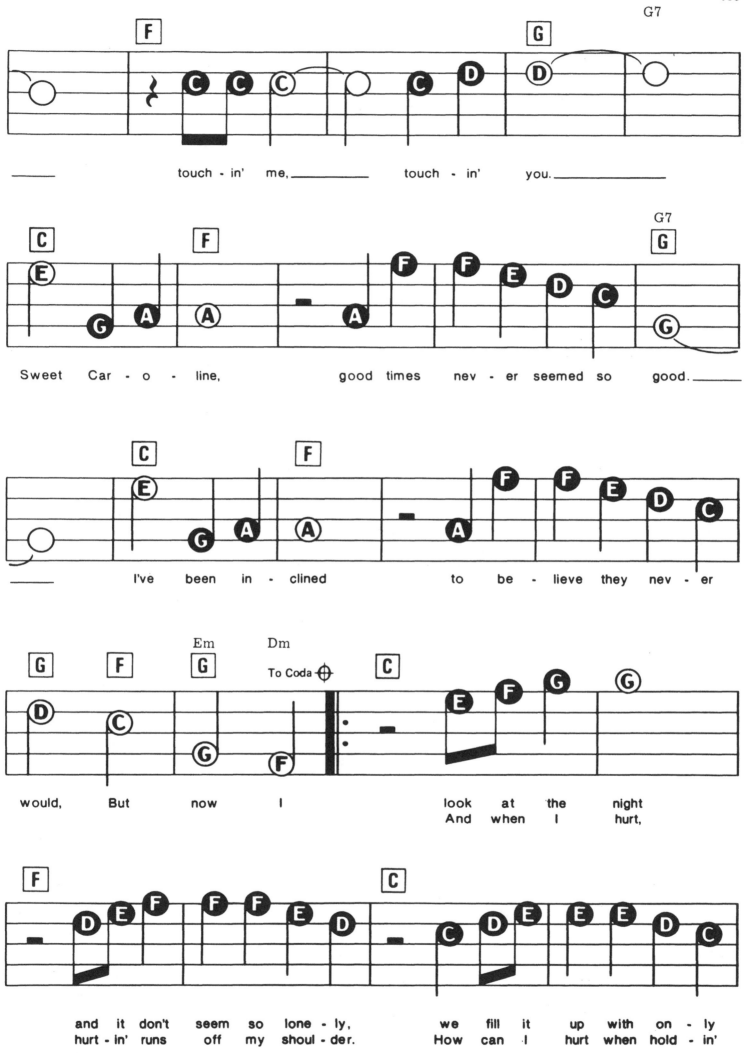

134

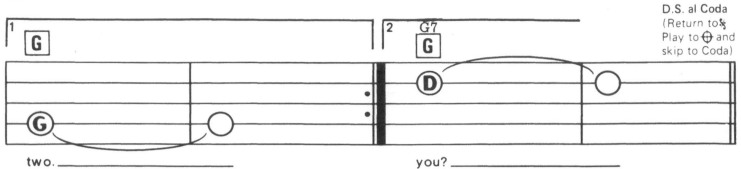

two. you?

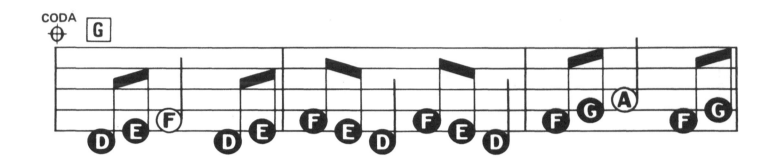

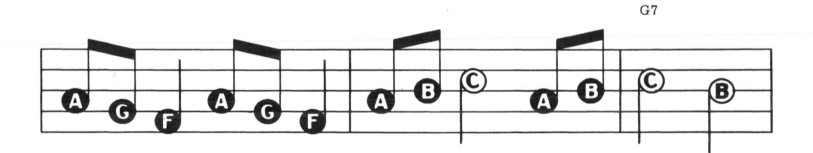

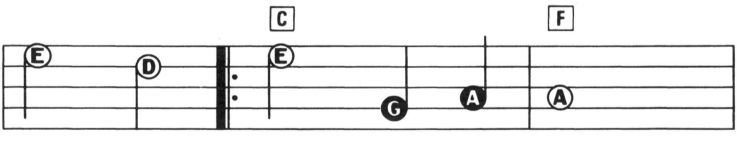

Sweet Car - o - line,

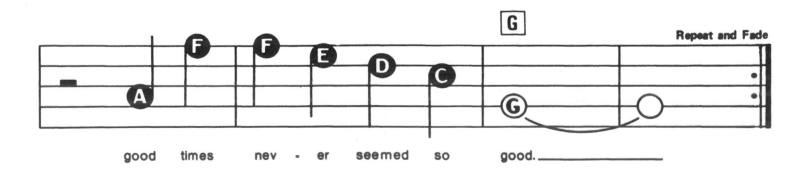

good times nev - er seemed so good.

You Don't Bring Me Flowers

Registration 4
Rhythm: Ballad or Fox Trot

Words by Neil Diamond,
Marilyn Bergman, Alan Bergman
Music by Neil Diamond

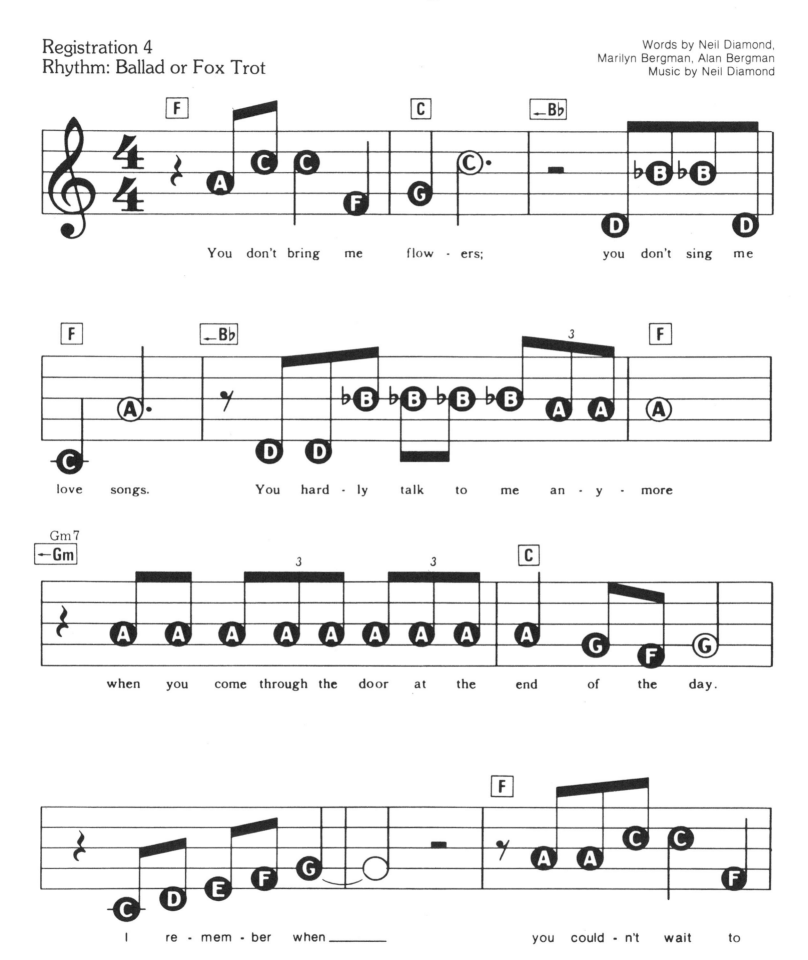

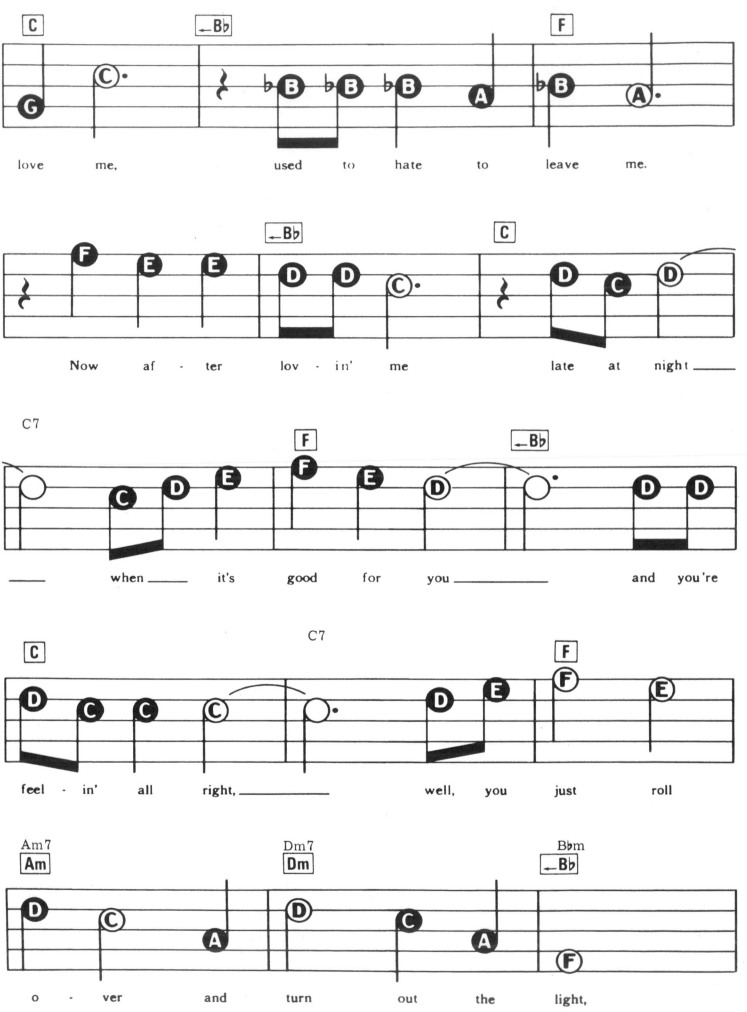

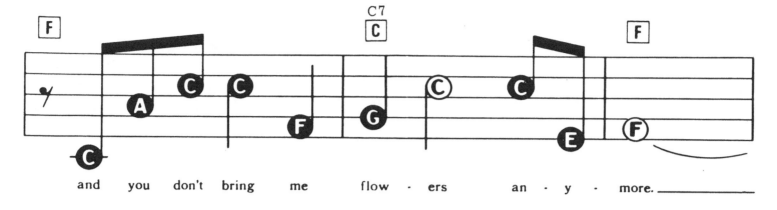

and you don't bring me flow - ers an - y - more. _____

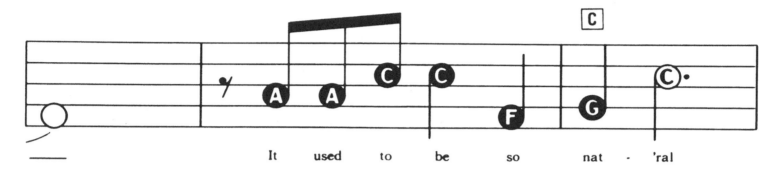

_____ It used to be so nat - 'ral

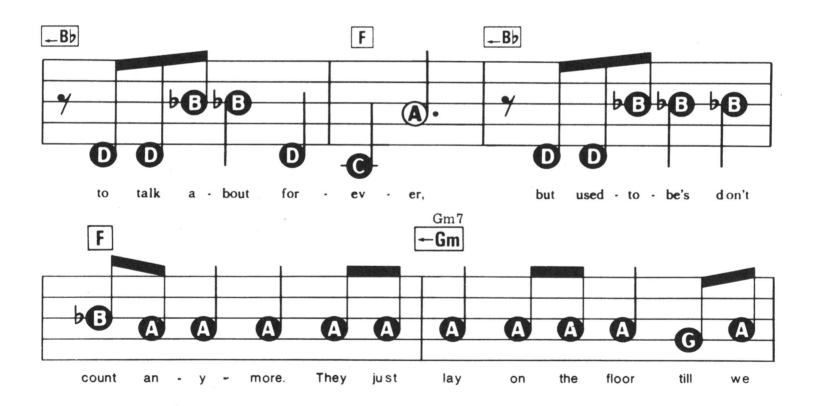

to talk a - bout for - ev - er, but used - to - be's don't

count an - y - more. They just lay on the floor till we

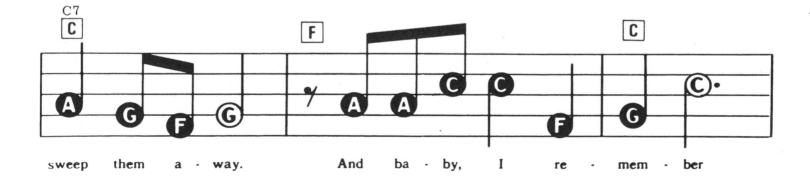

sweep them a - way. And ba - by, I re - mem - ber

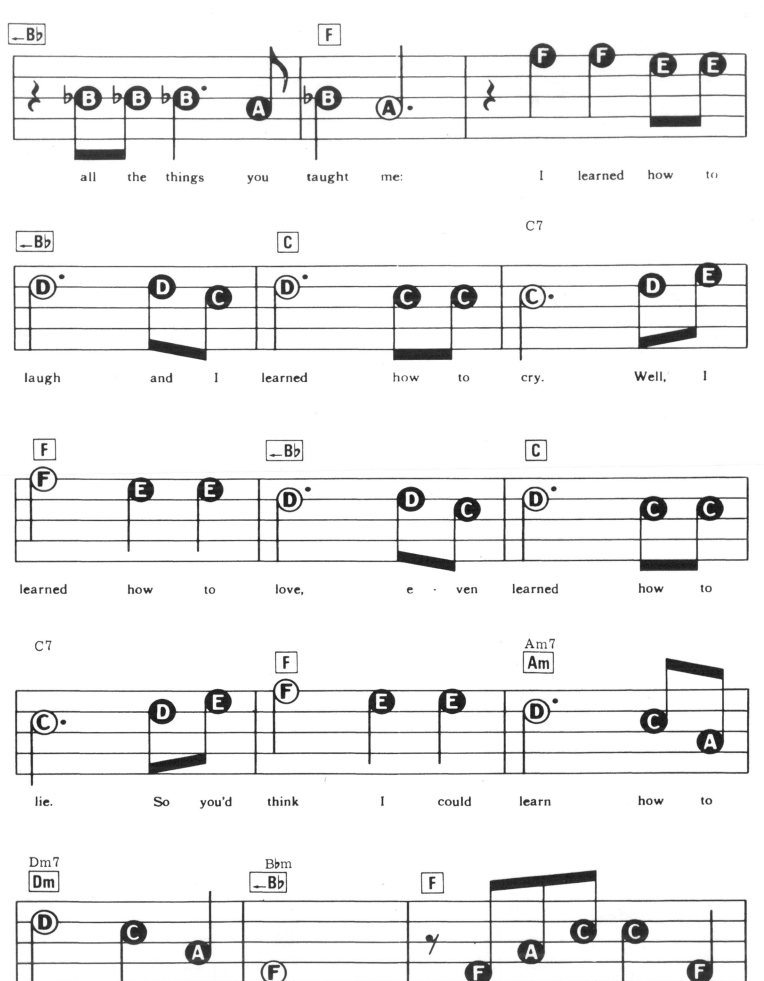

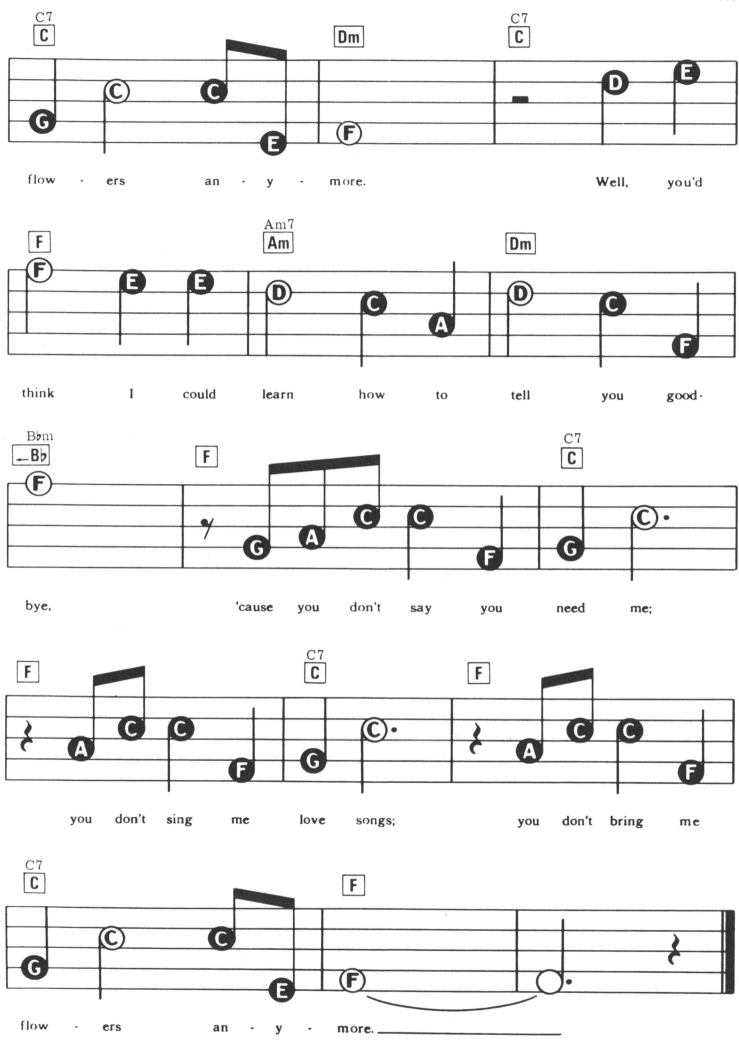

Thank The Lord
For The Night Time

Registration 3
Rhythm: Ballad or Fox Trot

Words and Music by
Neil Diamond

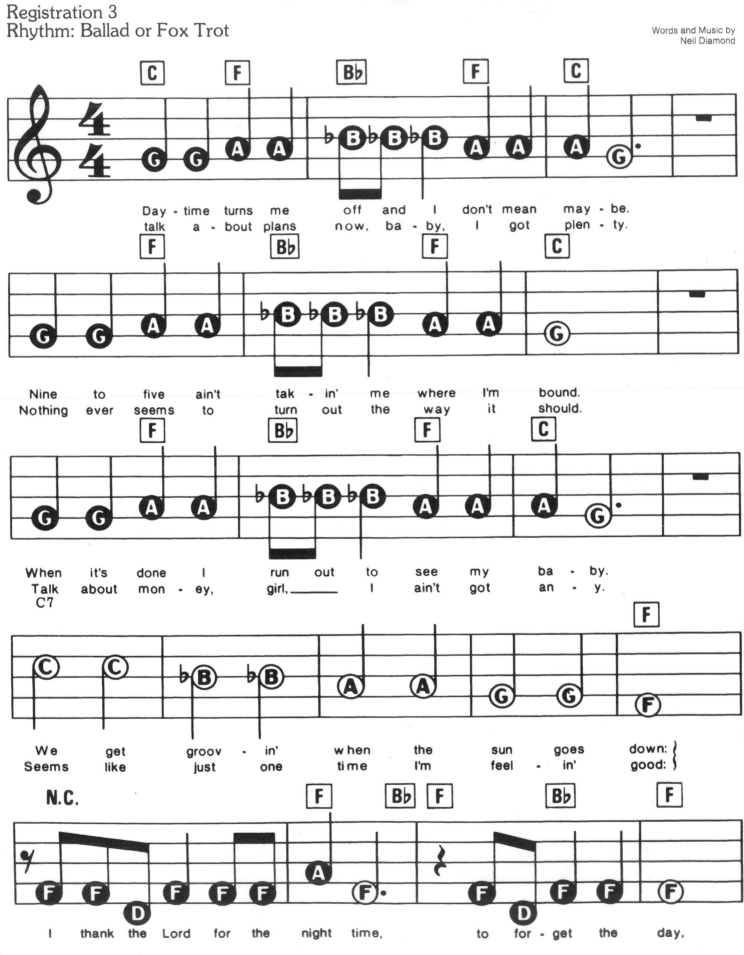

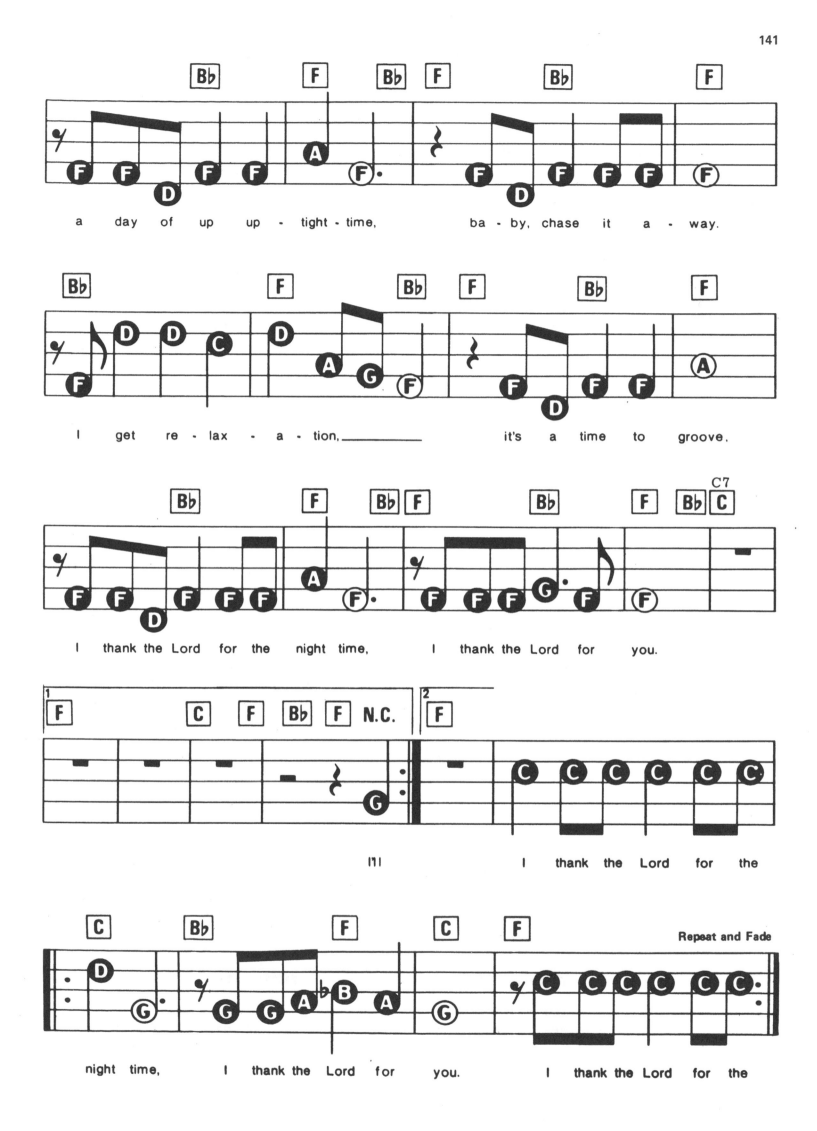

Yesterday's Songs

Registration 4
Rhythm: Ballad or Country Western

Words and Music by Neil Diamond

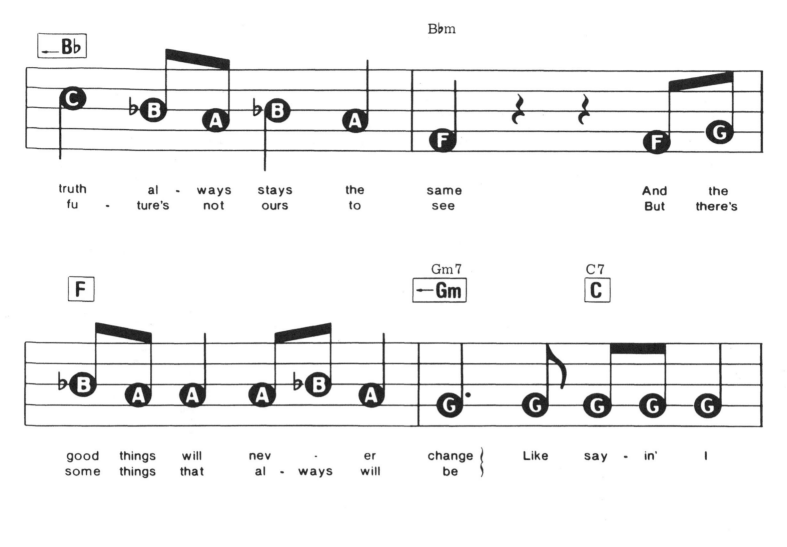

truth   al - ways   stays   the   same   And   the
fu - ture's   not   ours   to   see   But   there's

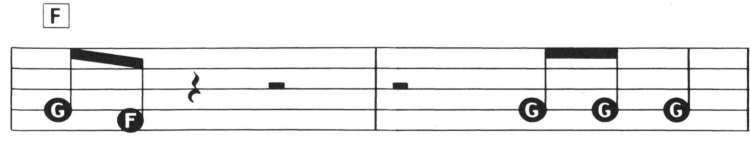

good   things   will   nev - er   change {   Like   say - in'   I
some   things   that   al - ways   will   be {

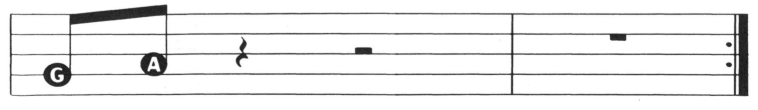

love   you   Say - in'   I

love   you

E-Z Play® TODAY Registration Guide
For All Organs

On the following chart are 10 numbered registrations for both tonebar (TB) and electronic tab organs. The numbers correspond to the registration numbers on the E-Z Play TODAY songs. Set up as many voices and controls listed for each specific number as you have available on your instrument. For more detailed registrations, ask your dealer for the E-Z Play TODAY Registration Guide for your particular organ model.

REG. NO.		UPPER (SOLO)	LOWER (ACCOMPANIMENT)	PEDAL	GENERALS
1	Tab	Flute 16', 2'	Diapason 8' Flute 4'	Flute 16', 8'	Tremolo/Leslie – Fast
	TB	80 0808 000	(00) 7600 000	46, Sustain	Tremolo/Leslie – Fast (Upper/Lower)
2	Tab	Flute 16', 8', 4', 2', 1'	Diapason 8' Flute 8', 4'	Flute 16' String 8'	Tremolo/Leslie – Fast
	TB	80 7806 004	(00) 7503 000	46, Sustain	Tremolo/Leslie – Fast (Upper/Lower)
3	Tab	Flute 8', 4', 2⅔', 2' String 8', 4'	Diapason 8' Flute 4' String 8'	Flute 16', 8'	Tremolo/Leslie – Fast
	TB	40 4555 554	(00) 7503 333	46, Sustain	Tremolo/Leslie – Fast (Upper/Lower)
4	Tab	Flute 16', 8', 4' Reed 16', 8'	Flute 8', (4) Reed 8'	Flute 8' String 8'	Tremolo/Leslie – Fast
	TB	80 7766 008	(00) 7540 000	54, Sustain	Tremolo/Leslie – Fast (Upper/Lower)
5	Tab	Flute 16', 4', 2' Reed 16', 8' String 8', 4'	Diapason 8' Reed 8' String 4'	Flute 16', 8' String 8'	Tremolo/Leslie
	TB	40 4555 554 Add all 4', 2' voices	(00) 7503 333	57, Sustain	
6	Tab	Flute 16', 8', 4' Diapason 8' String 8'	Diapason 8' Flute 8' String 4'	Diapason 8' Flute 8'	Tremolo/Leslie – Slow (Chorale)
	TB	45 6777 643	(00) 6604 020	64, Sustain	Tremolo/Leslie – Slow (Chorale)
7	Tab	Flute 16', 8', 5⅓', 2⅔', 1'	Flute 8', 4' Reed 8'	Flute 8' String 8'	Chorus (optional) Perc Attack
	TB	88 0088 000	(00) 4333 000	45, Sustain	Tremolo/Leslie – Slow (Chorale)
8	Tab	Piano Preset or Flute 8' or Diapason 8'	Diapason 8'	Flute 8'	
	TB	00 8421 000	(00) 4302 010	43, Sustain	Perc Piano
9	Tab	Clarinet Preset or Flute 8' Reed 16', 8'	Flute 8' Reed 8'	Flute 16', 8'	Vibrato
	TB	00 8080 840	(00) 5442 000	43, Sustain	Vibrato
10	Tab	String (Violin) Preset or Flute 16' String 8', 4'	Flute 8' Reed 8'	Flute 16', 8'	Vibrato or Delayed Vibrato
	TB	00 7888 888	(00) 7765 443	57, Sustain	Vibrato or Delayed Vibrato

NOTE: TIBIAS may be used in place of FLUTES.
VIBRATO may be used in place of LESLIE.